G – FOR GOD ALMIGHTY
A Personal Memoir of Lord Beaverbrook

Also by David Farrer
A CAREER FOR THE GENTLEMAN
THE SKY'S THE LIMIT

G - FOR
GOD ALMIGHTY

A Personal Memoir
of Lord Beaverbrook

DAVID FARRER

THE RYERSON PRESS — TORONTO

SBN 7700 0285 4

Printed in Great Britain

For Mollie Beales
in gratitude and affection

Contents

FOREWORD

I MUST make clear that this book is in no sense an attempt at a biography of the late Lord Beaverbrook. This is already being written by an historian of great eminence. It is not even a biography of the six and a half years of his life, from March 1940 to September 1946, during which I worked for him. It is what its sub-title states, a 'personal memoir', a worm's eye view of the most remarkable man with whom I have come in close contact.

Lord Beaverbrook became during his life to many almost a symbol of evil, and to others the object of great devotion. Had I to place myself in either camp it would be in the latter. The object of this book however is to portray him neither as saint nor sinner but as a human being. My only excuse for attempting this task is that at the apex of his career I was in almost daily touch with him and saw him in his every mood. *G – for God Almighty* might possibly find a tiny niche as a footnote to history. For of one thing I am convinced, history will accord a prominent place in the first half of the twentieth century to the subject of this book.

I am grateful to all those who have helped to refresh my memories of the times of which I write. Specifically I would like to mention Mr Albert Nockels and, above all, Mr George Malcolm Thomson, my senior colleague during the years of which I write. The reason for my deep gratitude to the latter will, I hope, be obvious to anyone who reads the book; he bears no responsibility at all, however, for my interpretations of the events in which we both took part.

My thanks are due also to my British publisher, Mr George

Weidenfeld who commissioned me to write the book; to Mr Sol Stein, my American publisher who in a mood of insane optimism bought the American rights after reading one chapter; to Messrs Cassell and Co. for allowing me to quote passages from Sir Winston Churchill's *The Second World War;* to Messrs Collins and Co. for permission to quote from the *Diaries and Letters* of Sir Harold Nicolson; and lastly to my old friend Sir Terence Creagh-Coen, in whose delightful Tangier home most of this book was written.

David Farrer
1969

I

FIRST MEETING

ONE EVENING early in March 1940 an old Oxford friend telephoned to me. His opening remark was: 'Would you like a job with Beaverbrook?'

'Good God, no!'

'It might be amusing.'

'You know what I feel about Beaverbrook.'

'But still – '

I hesitated, then curiosity got the better of me. 'Why on earth should he want to offer *me* one?'

'He's asked Tom to find him someone who was at Oxford to be his social secretary.'

Tom was Tom Driberg, who was then still editing the William Hickey column in the *Daily Express*. He was its originator, and incomparably the best of a long line of such editors.

'I can think of nothing more ghastly.'

But the other end of the line was not to be gainsaid. 'After all, your present job is pretty dreary.'

This was eminently true. But I answered pompously: 'At least it's part of the war effort.'

If he snorted with derision I did not hear him. He went on: 'At least go and have an interview. It'll make a good story afterwards.'

I hesitated again, then told him I would ring him back. This I did a little later, grudgingly giving my consent to my name being put forward.

The next morning the General Manager of the *Daily Express*, E. J. Robertson, rang up and asked me to go and see Lord Beaverbrook at three o'clock that afternoon. He seemed shocked when

I told him the earliest I could manage was six o'clock the following evening. Mine was scarcely the normal reaction of young men summoned to the presence with the prospect of a job ahead. However, the later date was agreed.

In the intervening thirty hours I did not even consult any of my friends. I went on with my job in the cable censorship at the Ministry of Information. I had no intention of becoming social secretary to Lord Beaverbrook. I was just going along for the ride. Punctually I presented myself at the appointed hour at Stornoway House, Beaverbrook's mansion in a cul-de-sac off St James's Street, its windows facing onto Green Park.

The front door was opened by a small man in a lounge suit. His demeanour, as he greeted me, combined the cocky and the obsequious in roughly equal proportions. As later he sized up my position in the household cockiness, so far as I was concerned, became the rule, but at this moment he was uncertain of my status – past, present or future. With his master obsequiousness, I soon discovered, was the rule to his face, and racy and often bawdy comment behind his back. His name was Albert.

'His Lordship's waiting for you in the library,' Albert said, and opened the big double doors on the right of the hall.

It was then that I got my first surprise.

Though I had never seen him in the flesh I thought I knew exactly what Lord Beaverbrook looked like. But my impression had been derived almost exclusively from the brilliant cartoons of David Low in the *Evening Standard*. Low portrayed him as an almost puck-like character, with an impish grin, a huge head and a tiny body. The man who rose from a deep arm-chair in the far window to greet me had, it is true, a big head, but he was also a big man. Broad-shouldered, with strong arms, he was, I think, about five foot nine inches tall, though his build lessened the effect of height. He gave me a welcoming smile, but there was no hint of mischief in it. The impression the cartoonist had given me vanished forever as, in that first minute of our first meeting, I felt the magnetism of his personality; and before the interview was over I had received my first dose of his extraordinary power to charm, when charm was the order of the day.

Though he never admitted it to me I am certain that Beaverbrook too was initially surprised. In the short time before the charm began to work I had made clear, by my manner perhaps subconsciously, but by words specifically, that I didn't want the job he was offering me. I told him, for example, that my job in the cable censorship was part of the war effort (pomposity again) and that I would find it very hard to resign from it. Now, as head of the most successful newspaper organization in the country, Beaverbrook was far from accustomed to such an attitude in a prospective employee. Almost every young journalist in Fleet Street or the provinces wanted to be on his payroll. He may have regarded my attitude as some sort of challenge. In any event he ignored, or seemed to ignore, my opening gambit. The charm was switched on. After some introductory remarks, during which he thanked me for coming to see him, he asked me: 'Did Robertson' (phonetic spelling in other people's books always irritates me, but in Beaverbrook's Canadian accent an 'o' became a long 'a') 'and that fellow Driberg tell you about the job?'

'Yes, I gathered I was to be your social secretary, arrange your entertaining, dinner parties, that sort of thing.'

He paused, as if reflecting. Then: 'Nonsense. How could I give dinner parties when there's a war on, and,' he added, and for the first time I recognized the cartoonist's impishness, 'food rationing too.' (Later I was to find out how, though not as entertainments manager.)

'I see. Then what am I supposed to do?'

'I want a political secretary.'

'A *political* secretary?' That one word changed my whole attitude, opening up undreamed of vistas. Inwardly I turned from a surly watchdog guarding my supposed conscience and principles into a puppy eagerly accepting a bone.

'Yes. Read the newspapers, analyse them, learn to write political articles, leaders. Tell an old man what young men of your age are thinking.' He expatiated at some length, then finished by saying: 'I've never had a secretary who was at Oxford.'

Faux naif this last sentence may have been, but my initial reactions to this interview had by now been transmuted into near-euphoria. I swallowed it whole. What he wanted was a really educated secretary – *me*.

The conversation proceeded on more general lines. I was by now not only charmed but bemused. It was all so totally unexpected, the sudden prospect of becoming a political journalist, the flattery implied in Beaverbrook's attitude, the chance, who knows, of becoming a sort of *éminence grise*. Who cared about the cable censorship? He asked me about my background, my Oxford career, my present job. I answered almost automatically. Finally he asked me if I would like the job.

Why did I not immediately accept? What follows is certainly a truer explanation than the one I then gave to Beaverbrook. I told him I would like to think it over during the weekend, giving as the reason my job in censorship. He agreed to this. On reflection, I believe that, had I accepted at the end of this first meeting, my lot might subsequently have been cast in more difficult places. Without knowing it I had had the best of the first battle, mainly because he had not anticipated a battle of any kind. I only really had to fight one other.

But why he accepted the delay, when so many other young men would have jumped at the opportunity, I shall never know. Perhaps he liked, how ever feebly it was delivered, a challenge.

As I sat in my Bloomsbury flat that evening, it was obvious that Beaverbrook's offer might be the chance of a lifetime. And so far, up to the age of thirty-three, it had been a not unamusing but a singularly unproductive lifetime. It had started not badly. At my public school, Rugby, I had reached the exalted, and character-destroying, position of Head of the House, which meant in those days my being invested, at the age of eighteen, with an absolute power over other boys which even Hitler in his prime might have envied. I was also a skilful, though extremely cowardly, player of the game of Rugby football. Most important, I was blessed with a teacher of history whose skill in coaching boys into Oxbridge scholarships was unrivalled. His method was simple. If you did not know much about the question asked, you switched it to another subject on which he had coached you. It worked like this. Question: Give your opinion on the military and political tactics of Julius Caesar. One's answer began: 'In considering the career of Julius Caesar it is interesting to compare the career of the Emperor Charles V.' And so on. I have practised these tactics all my life.

Armed with this secret weapon, I scored an unexpected history scholarship at Balliol College, Oxford. But the real reason for this success was, I suspect, the fact that my family had been Balliol men for many generations and that my elder brother had won a history exhibition and later a 'first' in 'Greats'. The Balliol authorities took a calculated and, it turned out, miscalculated risk.

So far so good. But at Oxford I did very little work and became stage-struck. In three successive productions of the Oxford University Dramatic Society I played an earl, a duke and a prince. But despite these gentlemen's exalted stations in life only the prince had more than forty lines to speak. Small however as these parts were, they involved me to the hilt in rehearsals, social occasions, the glamour created by the arrival at Oxford of real life professional actresses to play the female leads. The inevitable result of all this was a very undistinguished 'second' in the history school.

My future at this stage was anyway predetermined – unless I had possessed far more strength of character, or had got a 'first', in which case offers, Civil Service or others, might have been made. My father had been a very successful barrister and my elder brother had joined the family firm of solicitors. Therefore I would become a barrister. I did, or rather I started the probationary period, known as 'eating my dinners', required before I could pass the necessary examinations and qualify to don a wig and accept briefs.

From the start I disliked the whole set-up; the musty tomes of recorded case law which formed the precedents on which lawsuits must be fought or settled; the feeling, which I still have, that the arguments propounded in cases concerning wills, property, contracts (the main concerns of the Chancery Bar at which I was to practise) not only lacked glamour but too often had little relevance to contemporary life. Above all I disliked the prospect, dinned into me by my father, that I must work not only through the legal terms, but all through the vacations as well, the only times when someone might possibly employ me. I wanted to spend these times travelling abroad, or acting in amateur dramatic societies.

Still, though I viewed the future with some dismay, there was nothing else I particularly wanted to do, except to become a star of the stage which, on the evidence of the earl, the duke and the prince, seemed unlikely. So I dutifully became a pupil in the chambers of a highly successful King's Counsel. My fellow pupils were Charles Russell and the late Aly Khan. Charles worked hard, and is now one of the most eminent and brilliant judges that even his remarkable family has produced. Aly Khan spent his time betting and taking a hand in the management of his father's – the Aga Khan's – enormous racing interests. I concentrated on writing a revue to be performed by amateurs for charity. Shades of the earl, the duke and the prince. We were the oddest trio.

It was therefore not surprising that, in order to pass the then very lenient bar examinations, I had to rely on a whispered conversation with my next door neighbour, who very courteously, and clandestinely, passed me his answer to a vital question. I was as a result called to the bar and entitled to advise eminent clients and, if necessary, appear in court. My brother did his best to supply me with briefs, but the results were disastrous. Twice I appeared in court, on each occasion I forgot my lines.

It took me about a year to discover how much I disliked the bar and how very bad I was going to be at it. It took me two more years before I braved my father by telling him so. The blow was softened when, almost simultaneously, I managed to get a job as a journalist (of sorts) with the Amalgamated Press and to have a novel accepted for publication. It had been written, of course, when I should have been studying my law books, and has never had a successor, the second novel being quite rightly rejected by most of London's publishers. The job carried the princely salary of three pounds a week. I was put to work on helping to compile a Concise Universal Biography. When finished it presented little challenge to the editors of the world-famous *Dictionary of National Biography*, from which indeed most of my own contributions were largely cribbed.

This job lasted two years. I then paid a visit to India, where in answer to an advertisement in the *Times of India* I found myself employed as tutor to the sixteen-year-old heir presumptive to the Maharajah of Gwalior, a state the size of Holland and Belgium combined. J. R. Ackerley's famous book *Hindoo Holiday*, describing his experiences in a similar capacity, had been published a year or two earlier, and I had visions of a princely salary and large 'perks'. But Ackerley had spoiled the market. My salary was modest and I was offered no bribes. Perhaps this was due to my lack of know-how. Certainly the atmosphere by which I was surrounded was one of almost medieval intrigue. After I had been in his employ for barely three weeks my employer, who was chief minister of the state, took me aside and asked me : 'Do you think my son is the sort of boy who will intrigue against me at the Palace?' My handsome young bearer (servant) was seduced in turn by my employer and by his fourteen-year-old daughter.

My task was to coach my pupil for the Oxford University Higher Certificate Examination ten months later. This involved, to start with, my re-learning *amo, amas, amat* in the morning and trying to make him learn it in the afternoon. The task in fact resembled a minor labour of Hercules and I never looked like successfully accomplishing it. I learned more about Indian history from him than he learned about anything from me. After I had returned to England he was sent to the British-run Princes College at Ajmer where he paid me the dubious compliment of being sacked for being anti-British.

Back in England after this colourful but unproductive interlude, I got another semi-journalistic job, helping to edit an early version of 'make-do and mend' books, this time at six pounds a

week. This started in April 1938 and lasted until the outbreak of
war, when I was wafted by the head of my department into the
newly formed Ministry of Information. The division of what, at
this time, was a gigantic white elephant which I found myself
in was headed by R. H. S. Crossman; it was probably the most
frustrating post he has ever held during a long and brilliant
career. We had no idea of what we were meant to be doing,
and no one told us. What they told me two months later was
that my services were no longer required. If this was a measure
of retrenchment, it failed in its purpose. I was almost
immediately offered a better paid job in another division of the
Ministry, the cable censorship.

As a junior censor I made a mark of sorts. In the early hours of
the morning, shortly after I had started the job, an outgoing
cable was placed on my desk in the office of Cable and Wireless
Limited for my attention. It read: 'Your 325783 Yes.' It seemed
harmless and I passed it. The next morning the closely guarded
Admiralty secret that the troopship Lancastria had been sunk
in the Irish Sea was revealed in the newspapers of the world.
How was I to know that the in-coming cable, to which this was
the answer, and which, for some obscure reason, we censors
were not at that time allowed to see, had asked precisely
that question? I survived this disaster and in March 1940,
unknown to me, had been recommended for promotion to a
higher grade.

So there was no successful career behind me, and certainly no
glittering prospects ahead, which might be jeopardized by
accepting Beaverbrook's offer. But as, that weekend, his
personal magnetism began a little to wear off doubts crept in.
'You know what I feel about Beaverbrook' had been my initial
reaction to the prospect of a job with him; and what I felt then,
before I met him, was acute dislike of all he seemed to stand
for. He had been, I argued, the arch-appeaser in the years before
the war and, I suspected, was still an appeaser now. His newspapers were brash, anti-culture of any sort; his gossip columns
– above all Lord Castlerosse's 'Londoner's Log' – reeked of

vulgarity. He was a political intriguer, his Empire Free Trade campaign was just a form of personal advertisement. These were views held at that time by the majority of my contemporaries and friends who, like me, had never met him, and are held even today by some of them, despite his record in war and peace. Certainly they were held by my parents.

Beaverbrook's antecedents and background are too well known to need description here – the son of an impoverished New Brunswick manse, the young dollar millionaire at thirty, etc. – My father and mother, to whom I was devoted, were what Burke calls 'Landed Gentry' and minor members, though the word had not then been coined, of the Establishment. My father had inherited a five-hundred-acre estate in Dorset; he was a local Justice of the Peace, a member of the Dorset County Council. My mother performed admirably the role of a country hostess – house parties for Hunt Balls, garden parties in aid of charities – though her heart was always in London whence she had been abruptly uprooted when my father left the Bar. My father called himself an Asquithean liberal but for the past twenty-five years neither he nor she had ever voted anything but Conservative. They admired Baldwin, distrusted Churchill (until the summer of 1940), considered Beaverbrook a totally bad influence on the country. They stood, in fact, for a great deal that Beaverbrook seemed constantly to be attacking. Hitler was worse and, so far as my mother was concerned, after she had been taken to a meeting of the Oxford Group, Dr Frank Buchman ran the Führer pretty close, but Beaverbrook was well up in the top ten of their dislikes.

To a very considerable extent I shared their attitudes and prejudices, though on Munich they agreed, perhaps for the first time, with Beaverbrook and I disagreed with them. Was it possible, given the total incompatibility of background, that I could ever work happily or successfully for a man whom I had been brought up so thoroughly to condemn?

Through the weekend I wavered. Then at a small lunch party on the Sunday I sat next to the famous Margot Asquith. I mentioned to her that I had been offered a job with Beaverbrook. It was, on the face of it, a foolish remark. Beaverbrook had been the chief architect of her husband's downfall when in the middle of the First World War Lloyd George supplanted him as Prime Minister. She turned to me and in a voice charged with venom said: 'If you take it, you'll put yourself completely beyond the pale.'

Somehow that clinched it.

Punctually at three o'clock on the Monday I presented myself at Stornoway House. Albert again opened the door, still uncertain what to make of me. Beaverbrook greeted me. He must have known what my re-appearance signified. 'Well?'

'I'd very much like to have the job.'

'Good. When can you start?'

'Technically, I've got to give a month's notice.'

'Try to make it sooner.'

'I don't think I'm as valuable to them as all that.'

He grinned. 'Start as soon as you can. Let Robertson know.' And with that complimentary valediction he showed me into the hall. 'Albert, get Mr Farrer a taxi.' He never gave that sort of instruction again.

It wasn't until an hour later that I realized that one very important matter had not even been mentioned. What was he going to pay me? Hastily I telephoned Tom Driberg at the Daily Express, to be told that he was in the country. I put through a long-distance call, and was answered by his house-keeper. 'Mr Driberg is in bed with the flu. He doesn't want to be disturbed.'

'Could you tell him it's very urgent?'

There was a long pause, then Tom's justifiedly peevish voice saying: 'I'm ill. What is it?'

'Tom, I'm terribly sorry. I've accepted the Beaverbrook job. What ought I to ask him as salary?'

'God! Five minutes ago he got me out of bed to ask me what *he* should offer *you*.'

The result was the largest salary I had ever been paid. And Tom made a rapid recovery.

2

GETTING TO KNOW YOU

IN RETROSPECT the first six weeks with my employer, from the last week of March until 14 May 1940, seem almost like a calm before the storm. They did not feel like that at the time. Getting to know Lord Beaverbrook was certainly exciting; it was also extremely alarming. When safely in his bottle this particular genie could be all smiles and affability. Then the cork would explode and unpredictability would take over. Ideas for leading articles would pour forth, his editors would tremble at the other end of the telephone, while I would frenziedly try to take down his instructions in wildly abbreviated longhand. Albert would be denounced – accused on one occasion of purloining six handkerchiefs. Arrangements would be hastily made in the morning for Beaverbrook to take the train for Paris and thence to his villa in the South of France, and cancelled the same evening. I soon realized how sheltered my previous existence had been. Even the vagaries of my Indian employer, asking me whether his son was a boy likely to indulge in self-abuse, were mere zephyrs compared with the contrary winds that now blew round my bewildered head. An Indian millionaire had, in the 1930s at least, a less frustratable life than his European counterpart.

Beaverbrook was indeed at the time he hired me – though I did not then realize it – in a mood of violent, if somewhat futile, frustration. Over the previous decade he had wielded considerable political influence. His campaign for Empire Free Trade had made little real sense, since it totally lacked the support of the majority parties in the Dominions. But it had had an appeal to the patriotism of right-wing Tories and had so dented the complacency of Stanley Baldwin, the Tory leader, as to provoke him into accusing Beaverbrook of wielding power without responsibility, 'the privilege of the harlot through the ages'. And in a rip-roaring, Beaverbrook-sponsored, by-election campaign, in the normally staid constituency of St George's Westminster, the Empire Free Trade candidate had come near to beating his official Tory opponent – while the Socialists looked amusedly on.

Empire Free Trade was followed by 'appeasement', and here again, paradoxically, Beaverbrook's campaign in his news-papers against involvement in Europe had the enthusiastic support of most right-wing Tories, a class whom in his heart he despised. 'There Will Be No War', the *Daily Express* was pro-claiming in banner headlines right up to the last days of August 1939.*

And then there *was* war, and Beaverbrook was not only apparently discredited but, as it were, out of a job. He had his newspapers, emblems of his journalistic genius, but there was now no political purpose to which he could put them, and, as he himself much later stated in his evidence before the Royal Commission on the Press, his newspapers were always to him means to political ends. On the political scene there was absolutely nothing for him to do – and he smarted too under the label of what had now become a dirty word – appeaser. Neville Chamberlain, the Prime Minister, sent him early in 1940 on an undefined mission to the United States. He was, it was understood, to drum up support among his friends, the American newspaper proprietors, for the British war effort. This was indeed a hard assignment, since this effort was at that time seemingly negligible. American support was likely only in the event of successes – or, as it proved, of almost total disaster. Beaverbrook's sense of frustration was in no way lessened by this American visit.

So, in March 1940, Beaverbrook was sulking in his tent. Stornoway House was, however, a very commodious, well-stocked, and hospitable tent. One of my first surprises was the

* Later in Noel Coward's war film, *In Which We Serve*, the opening shot was of a bedraggled *Daily Express* poster 'There Will Be No War' lying in the gutter. It was many years before Beaverbrook forgave him.

people who visited it. Sir Samuel Hoare could be expected, one of the arch-appeasers, and of course fellow-newspaper proprietors like Lord Rothermere. But what, on the right-wing of politics, of Duff Cooper, who had resigned over Munich, and earlier had been the official, anti-Beaverbrook candidate in the Empire Free Trade by-election? And what of the men of the Left? In my innocence I had imagined that to Socialists Beaverbrook, the arch-apostle of capitalism and free enterprise, must be anathema. Yet to the Stornoway tent came Maxton and McGovern of the far political Left and H. G. Wells, the greatest Utopian of them all. Little as I knew him then, I did know that Beaverbrook had been the close friend, and financial adviser of Rudyard Kipling. Kipling and H. G. Wells? I had a great deal to learn.

One of the first things I had to learn was that I knew nothing about the craft of journalism. Beaverbrook wasted no time in testing me in this field – I had made a point of stressing my jobs with the Amalgamated Press, and later with Odhams. Within a fortnight he had bidden me write an article for the *Evening Standard* on the subject of the National Debt. I was compelled to admit that this was a subject which had not previously exercised my mind. Staccato, he fired at me a number of facts and figures, then left me to it. I went to work with a will. In Mandarin-Oxford prose I weighed the pros and cons, every opinion was carefully qualified by phrases that all too often began 'Nevertheless'. All in all, I thought, a balanced survey of a subject about which I knew absolutely nothing. Within twenty-four hours I had delivered what I fondly believed was the finished article.

Disillusionment came the next morning. Beaverbrook handed me back my article. It was hardly recognizable. Gone were all my qualifications, gone those rolling periods, gone all the commas, not a sign of a semi-colon. The blue pencil reigned supreme. No paragraph, in the revised version, lasted more than six lines. Pungency was all; and in the English language as written by Beaverbrook's newspapers there was one unbreakable rule – if a sentence didn't begin with 'and' it should start with 'but'. Re-reading this article today, it seems to me riddled with fallacies and half-truths, as so much of Beaverbrook's thinking on the nation's finances always was, but to carry a punch that made an esoteric and abstruse subject highly palatable to a general reader. Little of this was due to me, and it was with mixed feelings that I saw it appear, under my name, two days later in the *Evening Standard*. Pride was mingled with a sense of false pretences.

Pride was uneasily reinforced the following evening. Frank Owen, the editor of the *Evening Standard*, paid a late visit to Stornoway House. We left together, and he asked me for a drink at a neighbouring public house. Over the first whisky he congratulated me warmly on my article. I answered gratefully, but warily. He had just seen the man who had made it publishable. But then in some way, over the second drink, he made it clear that he thought the article was my unaided work. 'The Old Man,' he said, 'was very pleased with it.' It was my first example of the generosity of spirit of which this astonishing man, for whom I was to work for the next six and a half years, could be capable.

Astonishment was, in those first days, my prevailing emotion. Hitherto routine had played a considerable part in my life. At home my father allowed his children, and his guests, to be a quarter of an hour late for breakfast at half past eight. One minute after that and one's entrance was greeted with the blackest of looks. In the evening a gong warned that dinner would be served in half an hour. Even as a reluctant, fledgling, barrister, I was punctual when arriving in the morning and even more punctual in leaving at night. In every job I had held I had been able to wake up in the morning with a fairly certain idea of what the day – and often the whole week – might hold. At Stornoway House there was no such certainty. There was only one fixture. I was required to arrive at nine o'clock, was presented with the daily papers and had to be prepared to achieve a summary of their leading articles half-an-hour later. After that the day's events were totally unpredictable, as was my hour of departure. Routine was a word, as many a civil servant was shortly to realise, that had been left out of Beaverbrook's vocabulary.

Sometimes he was dressed by the time my summary was prepared and I would discuss it with him in the library. More often I was required to ascend in the surprisingly old-fashioned lift to the top floor, there to find him in his bath, or sometimes perched on his lavatory seat. He was totally unembarrassed by his own nakedness.

'Good morning, Sir.'

'Anything going on?'

I can remember few occasions during the whole time I was with him when this was *not* his opening matutinal remark. In these early days it was usually supererogatory, he had already been on the telephone to the editor of the *Evening Standard* who had to be on duty by 7 a.m., but still – . There was an occasion fifteen months later, however, when I was caught napping. The date was Sunday, 22 June 1941, and unknown to me Beaverbrook had overslept. He telephoned me at about ten o'clock. 'Anything going on?'

'No, I don't think so.'

'Nothing at all?'

'Well – the Germans have bombed Minsk, Kiev and Leningrad.' – I said it almost as a throw-away line, having heard the news on the wireless two hours earlier.

'Wha-a-a-t?'

It was thus that Beaverbrook received his first firm news of the German invasion of Russia.

After the morning newspaper ritual was over anything might happen; a walk, twice round Green Park, a stream of notes to his editors, for articles that never got written, for speeches that never got made. Frequently we would just talk, or rather he would talk and I would anxiously listen, trying to keep pace with his bewilderingly rapid brain. Sometimes he would break off and ask: 'Don't you agree?' I am ashamed to admit that, though in those early days I frequently didn't, I never admitted to the fact. Likewise, when occasionally he asked *my* opinion on a subject I did my best to make it square with what I believed to be his own view. I was far too uncertain of my own position vis-à-vis this phenomenon, who had for undisclosed reasons chosen to employ me, to jeopardize it by any considerations of principle or belief. The strength of his personality seemed anyway to preclude argument with him. It was enough to be exposed to the force of it.

I was, those first six weeks, constantly on tenterhooks, but it would be untrue to say that I was overworked. Frequently, on the contrary, I had time on my hands. For this there was one very good reason. I was not the only personal secretary. The name of the man on whom I had been foisted as a colleague was George Malcolm Thomson.

There is a story that one lunchtime, after he had been out riding with Beaverbrook in Rotten Row – a torture to which I was never submitted – George Malcolm Thomson said to his friend Percy Cudlipp: 'I felt as if Beaverbrook was Napoleon and I was Marshal Ney.'

'Don't you,' Cudlipp replied, 'mean Marshal Yea?'

The riposte was quick and amusing, but as Cudlipp well knew, it was very wide of the mark. By the time I went to Stornoway House George had established himself as one of the very few in Beaverbrook's entourage who dared to say 'Nay', who could argue with him and quite often persuade him to change his mind. He had a quality of self-reliance, a robust faith in his own judgement, a pragmatic approach to problems, that appealed to all that was best in Beaverbrook. He came to acquire a unique position in Beaverbrook's esteem and held it right up to the day of his employer's death.

George had come south, with Cudlipp his fellow-Scot, to seek his fortune in Fleet Street nine years earlier. In due course Cudlipp had become editor of the *Evening Standard* and George had been acquired by Beaverbrook. He might well have resented my appearance on the scene – a potential cuckoo in the nest. Instead, from the start he constituted himself my mentor and protector, guiding my faltering steps past the many pitfalls that any relationship with Beaverbrook involved, instructing me how to cope with our master's varying moods, above all warning me of the perils of knuckling under. Without George's advice and support, I would certainly have fallen victim to that peril. The Old Man, he told me, loved to dominate, given half a chance he would become a bully, but, however much he used them, he never really respected those of his employees who succumbed to his bullying. 'When you feel affronted or put upon,' George advised, 'for God's sake answer back.'

It was George too who, by casting the mantle of his friendship over me, smoothed my early relations with Beaverbrook's court. This was divided in two sections, administrative and journalistic, but the sections had one thing in common. Within a minute of receiving a summons from their Emperor they would have dropped everything, however important, they were doing, and would be on their way to Stornoway House. It was a case of Their Master's Voice.

Head of the financial section was E. J. Robertson, General Manager of the *Daily Express*, a man of complete integrity, trusted by every member of the organization from Beaverbrook downwards. In business matters Beaverbrook would often defer to him; he was a sort of Lord High Chancellor, but in political matters an innocent abroad who on at least one occasion during the war give his master most damaging advice.

Master of the Emperor's Household was George Millar. This outwardly insignificant-looking man, sitting in his room on the third floor of the Daily Express building in Fleet Street, was charged with a hazardous and Herculean task. He had to control and manipulate the whole of Beaverbrook's allegedly eight million pound fortune, dispense his charity, remember, for example, the names of the considerable number of ladies who looked forward to the occasional cheque. But this was not all. He was responsible too for the management, staffing and upkeep of both Stornoway House and Beaverbrook's country house, Cherkley Court near Leatherhead. He was there for all to shoot at, and many were the fusillades directed at him, by irate housekeepers, plaintive ladies, and daily by Beaverbrook himself.

'Mr Millar, the new housemaid you sent me is hopeless.'

'Mr Millar, do you think His Lordship can possibly have forgotten?'

'*Millar*. The bathwater was cold, and Albert has lost my reading glasses. God damn it, can't I get any service?'

No wonder George Millar normally wore a harassed look. His ultimate reward, a directorship in Beaverbrook Newspapers Limited, was richly deserved. I never saw him lose his temper. Perhaps, vis-à-vis Beaverbrook, it would have been better if he occasionally had.

With the financial division of the Court, I had at first little to do, except to transmit, and if possible tone down, to Millar rude messages from the All Highest. With the journalists it was otherwise. Favourites, almost to the point of being court jesters, in March 1940, were undoubtedly the brilliant trio of Frank Owen, Michael Foot and Peter Howard – who were not long after to collaborate in writing that pungent attack on the men of Munich, *Guilty Men*. It was indirectly a bitter attack on the ideas harboured at that time by their employer. He loved it. All three worked for the *Evening Standard*, of which Frank Owen was the editor, all were on the closest personal terms with Beaverbrook. All might well have looked askance at the arrival of one with whom they might in due course have to share their master's ear. That instead they each gave me a warm welcome was due in part to the fact that George Malcolm Thomson had already done so, even more to their own innate generosity. Peter Howard was, in point of time of service, the junior. George Malcolm Thomson tells the story of how when Howard first joined Beaverbrook, the latter gave George the task of coaching him as a feature writer, only for him to find out that Howard was getting a better salary than he.

Two of these young men were in their wildly disparate ways to achieve fame. Frank Owen, odd man out, perhaps achieved his greatest reputation as editor of the *Evening Standard*. His turbulent, Welsh character, and his immense physical attraction for women, proved a handicap. Yet as, for a brief period, a Liberal MP, and as author of a fine biography of Lloyd George, he made a further mark. Michael Foot is today the only real radical left in British life. In this era of political mediocrity when both of the main parties bow down to the god of expediency, Michael Foot's passionate idealism shines like a flaming, if often perhaps misguided, beacon. He may yet inherit the mantle of the late Aneurin Bevan. He feels, where others fumble.

Peter Howard, the third of this brilliant trio, went a very different way. This powerfully built ex-Rugger blue fell, after Beaverbrook entered the Government without taking Howard with him as one of his aides, under the spell of a very different man, the late Dr Frank Buchman. In due course, he succeeded Dr Buchman as head of Moral Rearmament. In this position he became an extremely successful shepherd of a very large number of sheep.

Each of these men exemplified Beaverbrook's genius for picking talent, and, at least so far as Owen and Foot were concerned, his ability to retain the affection of former employees long after the parting of the ways.

In Arthur Christiansen Beaverbrook picked talent of a different nature which in a way came close to genius. 'Chris' was made editor of the London *Daily Express* at the age of twenty-seven. In twenty years under his editorship the newspaper's circulation increased from about 500,000 copies to over four million. Under Frank Owen's, and later Michael Foot's, editorship the *Evening Standard* came to be known as the 'West-End Parish Magazine'. It was hard-hitting – no paper owned by Beaverbrook could ever be otherwise – but it was highly civilized, its articles were written by men who had read widely and were sensitive to upper and middle class trends at Westminster, in the City, in café society, and its editors were allowed a wide freedom to express views which were not necessarily those of their master. This tradition has prevailed up to the present day. Chris, on the other hand, was allowed no views of his own. The *Daily Express* was Beaverbrook's far from secret political weapon. The banner of Empire Free Trade flew at its masthead, together, on occasions, with such odd companions as 'Appeasement' and 'Rearmament'. With this state of affairs Chris was content. He was not politically minded. He was, however, in the world of journalism a supreme technician. Under his aegis the *Daily Express* far outstripped its rivals in presentation and lay-out. It was easy to read, succinct and sensational; and it told its mass audience of unsophisti-

cated readers – with a sop to the intelligentsia in the form of
Osbert Lancaster's cartoons – exactly what they wanted to
hear. Herein lay Chris's greatest strength. The average *Daily
Express* reader in his spare time liked a flutter on the horses or
the dogs, a pint or two in his local pub, and with his wife a
good musical spectacular film or Tommy Trinder on the
wireless, an occasional excursion to Clacton-on-Sea. These were
the preferences too of the editor of the *Daily Express* – he even
had a house at Clacton. He could identify with his readers, and
his circulation soared.

These were the inner court which revolved round the Beaverbrook axis and with whom I came most frequently in contact.
All of them owed their start and much of their inspiration to
the man who hired them. All would agree that he was the
greatest teacher of popular journalism of his – or perhaps of all
– time. Standing somewhat apart, even aloof, was another
powerful journalistic figure. John Gordon, editor of the *Sunday
Express* since 1928, also wrote, and still writes, a weekly
column of mixed social and political content, which in those
days caused the hackles of all who were not on the extreme
right to rise and brought every left-wing reader to the verge of
apoplexy. Such, none the less, was the pungency of Gordon's
style that his column was compulsive if often hated reading up
and down the country. I never heard Beaverbrook even attempt
to dictate what should go into it, and when Gordon came to
Stornoway House or Cherkley it was by invitation, never by
command. Gordon was one of that rare species, a working
journalist who actively saved and invested money while he was
working. Reputedly very rich, he was the object of Beaverbrook's admiration and, I think, of his jealousy as well. Money
in the bank brings a sense of independence. Beaverbrook did
not like his employees to feel independent, however much at
intervals he gave them the illusion that such was the case.

These were the days when the 'phoney' war, which had lasted
since the collapse of Poland six months before, came
dramatically and disastrously to an end. Within days of
Neville Chamberlain's declaration to the House of Commons
that 'Hitler has missed the bus', the Führer had caught it with a

vengeance by successfully invading Denmark and Norway. Such was the confusion into which the Government and armed forces were thrown that the Prime Minister was induced to tell Parliament that the Germans had landed at Larvik when the landing had been at Narvik, five-hundred miles further north. The fiasco of the British attempt to save Norway followed rapidly. Rumours of the impending invasion of Holland and Belgium were thick in the air. Visitors to Stornoway House were many and varied: American newspaper correspondents; Canadian industrialists – among them Sir James Dunn for whom Beaverbrook found a temporary secretary, who twenty years later became the second Lady Beaverbrook; members of the Government, and back-benchers, Tory and Labour alike. The tempo of plotting and intrigue was quickening and I was frequently banished to a small bedroom at the top of the house.

But among the visitors there was one conspicuous absentee. On the eve of the war's outbreak Beaverbrook had advised his close companion of thirty years, Winston Churchill, *not* to join Chamberlain's government. Why should he be tarred with the brush of Chamberlain's almost certain failure to cope with a war situation? Let him stand aside and in the fullness of time the country would demand him as its leader. There was never a chance that the advice would be accepted and Beaverbrook must have known it. But in these April days it looked as if it had been well given. It was the Navy who were bearing the brunt of the blame for the Norwegian disaster, and Churchill was First Lord of the Admiralty. Whether the two men communicated with each other at this time I do not know. If so, it is unlikely that the Press Lord resisted the temptation to say to the politician 'I told you so'. Certainly there was no call in his newspapers for Churchill to take over.

As the skies of war darkened, so did Beaverbrook become more moody and irritable. His mounting frustration cast its shadow on all his entourage. None of us escaped. Albert the valet was chivvied from pillar to post. I suffered less than most for I had already begun to practise the art of making myself scarce when storms were brewing. It was then that I made the resolution, for example, never to answer my telephone once I had got home to my flat. I adhered to it all through the war. Then suddenly there were fresh plans for me to accompany him to his villa in the South of France. This time it was real. Train and boat reservations were made. I was hustled off to get my passport visa. The day fixed for our departure was 10 May 1940.

3

THE HOUSE THAT MAX BUILT

WHY WAS the visit to the South of France planned? By the end of April the scope of the Norwegian disaster was evident. Rumours were rife, not only of an impending German attack in the West, but of widespread Government changes at home. Political crises had been meat and drink to Beaverbrook ever since in a suite at the Hyde Park Hotel at a previous crisis in the nation's fortunes, he had plotted the downfall of Asquith at the end of 1916. Why pass up the chance once again to be a king maker? The stream of visitors to Stornoway House made it clear that such again might be his role.

The official reason given for the journey was his asthma. It was to be trotted out time and again for the next two years, and always it had, in varying degrees, a measure of validity. For Beaverbrook asthma equalled frustration, and was nonetheless a real affliction for that. But asthma was not the whole story. Beaverbrook loved luxury and the sun. To some extent the war had deprived him of the former, and, to someone who had for many years been able to find sunshine whenever he wanted it, the long winter of blackout had been a nightmare. The South of France beckoned seductively, and it might, he well knew, be the last chance.

Above all, with half his mind Beaverbrook wanted to dodge the obviously impending political crisis. His affection was for Churchill, whom anyway he considered the only possible war leader if it came to a fight to the finish. But up to 14 May 1940, the most important day in his life, he would have preferred a negotiated peace; and it was round Churchill that the crisis in Parliament was certain to revolve. In the Villa Capponcina at

Cap d'Ail he could surely avoid being involved in a situation where his heart was at variance with his head.

Events overtook him. On 7 May – four days before his and my passport visas expired – the Labour Party initiated a debate in the House of Commons on the conduct of the war. At once it was obvious that the Opposition had the support of a considerable section of the Tory party. Quoting Oliver Cromwell, Leo Amery, a Privy Councillor, and past Cabinet Minister, declared: 'Depart, I say, and let us have done with you. In the name of God, go!' Chamberlain reacted over-violently, calling upon his 'friends' to support him, thereby ensuring that many who had been undecided would desert him. The debate continued into the next day. When the vote was taken, despite an impassioned defence of the Government by Churchill, thirty Tories voted against, and a further sixty abstained. It became clear to everyone, except perhaps Chamberlain, that the reign of the Prime Minister was at its end.

9 May was a day of febrile political activity, as the numerous memoirs and biographies of the period make clear. Certainly this activity had spread to Stornoway House. The telephone was in constant, conspiratorial use. In particular, communication between Stornoway and Admiralty Houses was fully and dramatically resumed. There was, alas! no means by which I could listen in, but the atmosphere left me in no doubt that we should *not* be going to the South of France. With the possibility, or rather the likelihood that Churchill would become Prime Minister, Beaverbrook's heart took over from his head. With Churchill at the helm it would be war *à l'outrance*. Never mind. He had for him a greater admiration and affection, however much their attitudes might in peacetime vary on public affairs, than for any other living man. All his efforts in those two days of May were devoted to the Churchill cause.

The morning of 10 May made it quite certain that we should not be going to France. The German armies invaded Holland and Belgium. On that same morning Chamberlain asked Lord Halifax, the Foreign Secretary, and Churchill to 10 Downing Street. Churchill has himself described the scene. 'Usually I talk a great deal, but on this occasion I was silent.'* Years later Beaverbrook told me that it was on his urgent advice that silence was preserved. The only way in which Churchill, so long the thorn in the side of the official Conservative Party, could be deprived of the Premiership was by demanding it.

That same evening Churchill became Prime Minister and started to form the new Government. He has, in the second volume of *The Second World War*, graphically described the process. 'The greatest difficulty was with Lord Beaverbrook.' The phrase is, to those who were at Stornoway House at the time, a generous understatement. Two years later, when Beaverbrook was temporarily out of office, I wrote an account of his time as Minister of Aircraft Production. The facts in that book have not been controverted; the interpretations of his actions owed perhaps more to the subject than to the author.

The offer of the newly to be created post of Minister of Aircraft Production was made on the morning of 11 May. He finally accepted it three and a half days later. In my book I described how 'to his personal secretaries Beaverbrook protested with increasing vehemence that he would not take office, and with each protest the secretaries became more certain that he would.' So far as I was concerned, with only six weeks' experience in his employment, I had no such certainty. The atmosphere at Stornoway House bordered on the hysterical. Beaverbrook behaved like a prima donna who, kept waiting for long in the wings, proclaims that the role is totally unsuitable and means that it is not the *leading* part. Was he, in fact, just playing hard to get? Had he any intention of refusing the position offered to him? In my view he was in doubt up to the moment of acceptance. In the brief interlude that heralded the transformation of a newspaper proprietor into a Cabinet Minister he had a very difficult decision to take. For many years he had been an absolute dictator in his special field. No one in the Express organization would dare seriously to cross his path. Now he was asked to assume a co-operative role as a member – however important – of a collective team led by a man who,

* Winston S. Churchill, *Their Finest Hour* (Vol. II of *The Second World War*), London and Boston, 1949.

he well knew, would himself prove a dictator in all but name.
Could he possibly make the transition? In the criticisms that
have subsequently been levelled against Beaverbrook's actions
as a Minister of the Crown this factor has never been given
sufficient weight. He was totally unversed in the arts of compromise. In many ways he was a political animal, but he was
never a politician.

So this very reluctant horse had been led to the water. To what
extent could he be persuaded to drink? The answer came
speedily. He drank avidly, in great gulps, almost to the point of
intoxication. In Stornoway House a sort of planned chaos came
into operation out of which, to everyone's surprise, a fully-
fledged Ministry began quickly to emerge. Beaverbrook had to
start from scratch. He had neither a staff nor a building in which
to house them. For the staff there was no lack of unofficial
applicants. From our top-bedroom eyrie, Thomson and I
watched a stream of callers, many of whom had in the preced-
ing years featured in Castlerosse's *Sunday Express* gossip column. They bore bizarre socialite nicknames like 'Scatters' or
'Skipper'. A few of them were taken on the strength with undefined duties. Only one of these amateurs survived for any length
of time. The Beaverbrook they now served was a very different
man from their host at Cherkley or companion at Claridge's or
the Café Royal in peacetime days. The survivor was Lord
Brownlow, a leading figure during Edward VIII's abdication and
now to be appointed Beaverbrook's Parliamentary Private
Secretary. In this position he suffered a measure of harassment
at his master's hand, which drove him finally into resignation
and the comparative shelter of the Lord Lieutenancy of Lincoln-
shire.

In the middle of these frenetic comings and goings there
appeared one sad figure. Sir Samuel Hoare had been sacked as
Secretary of State for Air and was to be banished to what then
looked like the outer darkness of the British Embassy in Madrid.*

* Where later he performed yeoman service in persuading Franco
to remain neutral.

He paid a farewell visit to Stornoway House, and on leaving, dropped a letter he had just received from a close colleague who, because of his vast experience in the mechanism of government, had survived the semi-purge of the old Chamberlain hands who had consistently opposed everything which Churchill had advocated. Albert picked up the letter, passed it to me, delighted at the prospect of mischief ahead. I copied it before returning it to Albert for onward transmission to its receiver. It read as follows:

My dear Sam:

I could not believe my ears or eyes when I learned that you were leaving the Air Ministry, where you were doing such magnificent work.

God help the country which, at the beginning of the supreme crisis of its fate, suddenly replaces half of the eight key leaders by men without experience of war or of public affairs (other than very sordid politics) or of administration, most of whom have consistently opposed all war preparation, and which commits its future existence to the hands of a dictator whose past achievements, even though inspired by a certain amount of imagination, have never achieved success.

But that the man who has mastered the problems of the key service of all should be replaced by an untried and wholly inexperienced politician, and who has made no mistake and shown how to combine initiative and daring with prudence – well it just beats the band.

I found complete chaos this morning. No one was gripping the war in its crisis. The Dictator, instead of dictating was engaged in a sordid wrangle with the politicians of the Left about the secondary offices. N.C. was in a state of despair about it all.

The only hope lies in the solid core of Churchill, Chamberlain and Halifax, but whether the wise old elephants will ever be able to hold the rogue elephant, I doubt.

The letter was in its way the swan-song of the Men of Munich.

Of very different calibre from the 'Scatters' and 'Skippers' and indeed from Sir Samuel Hoare were the 'professionals' – the civil servants – who were summoned to Beaverbrook's assistance. From the Air Ministry came Sir Charles Craven and Sir Wilfred Freeman, and from the Treasury, to head the Civil Service side of the new Ministry, Sir Archibald Rowlands. These three men of formidable character and talents were the foundations on which the Ministry of Aircraft Production (known rapidly to all concerned as MAP) must be built. Beaverbrook was fortunate in finding them, scarcely less fortunate in the two civil servants appointed to run his private office. Accustomed to the strict, unvarying rules of civil service procedures – you were allowed a carpet in your room only when you had achieved a certain rank and salary – Edmund Compton and John Eaton Griffiths could be excused for being at first very much fish out of water in the overflowing tank of Stornoway House. They learned to swim with remarkable rapidity. Perhaps they were helped a little by the two strange alien creatures with whom they were required to collaborate. Who were we, this Thomson and this Farrer? What were we up to, these interlopers from Fleet Street? Were we spies for the Minister? – (Beaverbrook did at first show some desire for us to assume that role – a tendency promptly and successfully resisted by Thomson.) Very soon, however, Whitehall and Fleet Street became firm allies, on occasions against the extraordinary man who was their master. On one occasion Compton asked Thomson to give him lessons in writing letters in Beaverbrook-ese.

Compton I had known before. We had been together at school at Rugby where, though he was intellectually far my superior, I was preferred to him, as the better games player, as head of our mutual House. Since then he had pursued a more orthodox and far more successful career than I, and so it has continued. He is today Sir Edmund Compton and well-known as Britain's first Ombudsman. Since his retirement, as Secretary of the Lawn Tennis Association, Eaton Griffiths, the other civil servant, has been one of the most active forces in admitting professionals to Wimbledon and other tennis tournaments.

Such were the admirable foundations on which Beaverbrook could build. But the question remained, what sort of house would be the house that Max built? Despite the strong foundations, there were formidable difficulties. Churchill's decision to create a Ministry involved a surgical operation on an existing one. The comparison with a heart, or at least, a kidney transplant was very close. The control of a whole department, development and production, was transferred from the Minister for Air, the newly appointed Sir Archibald Sinclair, together with its joint heads, Craven and Freeman, to Beaverbrook. Inevitably these men suffered a conflict of loyalties, between the admirable and orthodox colleagues they had left behind and the unpredictable man they now worked under. The situation was rendered no easier by the fact that the very creation of MAP implied a criticism of the Air Ministry's efficiency. This ruffled the feathers not only of high Air Ministry officials but, by association, of the new Minister himself. Sir Archibald Sinclair and Lord Beaverbrook were always Archie and Max to each other, but there was little real love lost between them.

These cracks in the structure were not helped by Beaverbrook's own lack of experience in dealing with civil servants. Though they were to a large extent papered over by the sense of national emergency, they existed none the less and on one occasion early in Beaverbrook's reign threatened real disaster.

Beaverbrook and Sir Archibald Rowlands, his Permanent Secretary, had a vigorous disagreement over a matter of policy. The Minister reacted as if Rowlands were one of his editors. He gave orders, assumed they would be carried out and thought no more about it – until the next day he received Rowlands's letter of resignation. On all counts Beaverbrook had miscalculated. Not only was Rowlands in this instance in the right, not only was he a dedicated civil servant, he was a Welshman with a quick temper who gave not a damn for anyone. Just in time Beaverbrook realized his mistake. George Malcolm Thomson was summoned, bidden to take a taxi post-haste from the Ministry, recently established on the Thames Embankment, to Stornoway House, there to collect a case of champagne and of whisky, with which he was to return and which he was

personally to deliver to Rowlands's private office with the com-
pliments of the Minister. The crates safely deposited, with the
taxi driver's help, outside the door, Thomson told Rowlands's
private secretary he had an urgent message from the Minister
to deliver, only to be told that the Permanent Secretary was in
conference. 'Can't I,' said the private secretary, 'deliver the
message?'

'I'm afraid you can't,' said Thomson, resisting the temptation
to add, 'It's too heavy.'

'Well, I'm afraid you'll have to wait.'

In due course the conference broke up and Thomson was
ushered into Rowlands's room. 'Well, where is this urgent
message?'

'It's outside the door.'

'What sort of message do you leave outside doors?'

'I'll show you.'

Rowlands observed the crates for a moment in silence. Then
he said: 'Tell the old bastard I won't touch a drop till the war's
been won. But meanwhile let's open a bottle of the champagne.'

But above all, the problem facing Beaverbrook in building his
new Ministry was one of speed. The previous Government had
made their production plans on the assumption that the war
would be long and apparently leisurely. The blitzkrieg in Poland
had done nothing to shake its complacency. On Chamberlain's
own confession, achievement of maximum war strength had
been planned for the middle of 1942. Within a week of Beaverbrook's appointment events in France had made it clear that
every possible gun, tank, and above all aircraft would be needed
not in two years' but at the most in two months' time. This was
no time for planning but for the scrapping of existing plans.
In the face of the situation's express urgency, the risk that the
new Ministry might be in part jerry-built must be accepted.
There was, for example, the problem of Harrogate. In pur-
suance of the policy of dispersal adopted when the war began
the Air Ministry's production departments, now transferred to
MAP, had been evacuated to this salubrious Yorkshire spa.

Beaverbrook wanted them back; not only his colleagues but his subordinates must be on the spot. Officialdom was vigorously opposed; their return would be against accepted policy and would cause administrative difficulties. Beaverbrook got his way, and so made it impossible for him to continue to run his Ministry from Stornoway House, which I believe he had in his heart wanted to do. He could consult his chief colleagues there, hold his Council meetings in the ornate first-floor ballroom whose doors were flanked suitably by flying cherubim, interview leading industrialists in the library where he first interviewed me, but even the imposing – and extremely ugly – mansion that was Stornoway House was not large enough to house two whole departments.

So a new home had to be, and was, found. It was the headquarters of Imperial Chemical Industries, facing the Thames where the river is crossed by Lambeth Bridge. Into this building the Ministry moved, Minister and all, a month after its formation.

It was, however, at Stornoway House that the early, the vital decisions were taken, the priorities decided, the able young industrialists who were to play so large a part in the near-miracle that was to follow enlisted. Twenty-eight years later I can still vividly recall the sense of extreme tension and excitement that in those days of dawning peril Beaverbrook single-handed created.

He was a master at creating this sort of environment. He thrived on the bullying, immediate, emotional approach to any problem. It was on his contempt for the orthodox that the success of his newspapers had been built. Now, such was the emergency, such the backing Churchill gave him, that for a brief period he had the chance to employ his unorthodoxy to the fullest extent. Stornoway House in the first month was its epitome. The house was a study in perpetual motion. No fixed hours, his Council summoned as the spirit moved him, added to by surprising and in this initial stage highly successful appointments. Often the most important decisions were taken across the dinner table – cold chicken and Alsatian wine. Later, reports would come in by telephone from assembly plants, engine factories. Upstairs Thomson and Farrer would doze fitfully, then, perhaps at one in the morning : 'Farrer (or Thomson), send a telegram, tell the Vickers people I congratulate them.'

'Which Vickers, Sir ?'

'God damn it, *Weybridge.*'

The emergency ? Dunkirk and, a fortnight later, the complete collapse of France. A Britain virtually denuded, except for the Navy, of defence. Above all, desperately short of aircraft without whose support the Navy would be unable to prevent a Channel crossing, and whose absence might lay Britain's cities open to complete devastation from the air. The methods Beaverbrook adopted to meet the emergency can be summed up in three words : 'the personal touch.'

Beaverbrook had emerged from the shadows of inactivity into the full sunshine of publicity. Within a few weeks of his Government appointment he was, after Churchill, the most talked-about man in the country. News of his activities spread rapidly. How, for example, he had challenged and vanquished the mighty Lord Nuffield, Director General of Aircraft Maintenance at the Air Ministry, stripping him of his powers, bringing his Shadow Factory under MAP control; how he was promoting industrialists hitherto unknown to the public to leading positions in his Ministry. They might lack seniority, they possessed in Beaverbrook's eyes drive and ruthlessness. Prominent examples of these new men were Patrick Hennessy and Trevor Westbrook.

Hennessy in May 1940 was in his thirties and general manager of Fords at Dagenham. Beaverbrook put him in charge of the entire materials side of MAP. Tall, sandy-haired, Hennessy spoke with a deceptively lazy Irish brogue. Within a very short time he had implemented new plans which doubled the production of those vital components of aircraft, aluminium and magnesium. Westbrook, put in complete charge of the repair of damaged aircraft, had a reputation already as a difficult, hot-tempered man, who had recently, as manager of a big bomber factory, quarrelled with its director and been summarily dismissed. In him Beaverbrook found an invaluable ally in his running battle with the mandarins at the Air Ministry whom he labelled collectively 'the Air Marshals'. Both men revelled in these fights, heedless of the embarrassment they caused to MAP's own Air Marshal, Sir Wilfred Freeman, the Ministry's Controller of Development. Their accompaniment was a constant flow of Minutes to the Prime Minister, many of which I had to draft. They followed an invariable pattern. 'My dear Prime Minister, I want,' then followed a list of what he did want, and then the peroration which ran something like this: 'If I am to continue to serve under your banner, it is essential that I be master in my own house.' Since Churchill was at that time in no mood to deny his old friend anything he wanted, the Air Ministry became in a short space of time the junior partner of MAP. The resultant friction between men and departments who had willy-nilly to work in close co-operation was harmful. More harmful would have been a continuation of the lack of drive and foresight which the 'Air Marshals' had previously displayed. Beaverbrook was too ruthless, but it was a time for ruthlessness.

It was as a peripheral part of Hennessy's drive for aluminium that I was given my first Governmental job. Beaverbrook launched a personal campaign: 'Send me your pots and pans, send me your aluminium.' At first in a trickle and rapidly in a flood these household utensils came pouring into the Ministry. They had, of course, to be acknowledged, and an ordinary Ministry would have evolved a stereotyped letter of thanks signed by whatever junior secretary happened to be available. But MAP was not an ordinary Ministry and Beaverbrook was a highly idiosyncratic Minister. He believed in the personal touch. Every donor must have a personal letter signed by the Minister, and each letter must be different. To me was allotted the duty of drafting them. It was an arduous task. The phraseology needed for a Viscountess was very different from that which a three-year-old child might be expected to enjoy. Baby Keith Whitfield was a case in point. Not unnaturally he did not actually possess an aluminium pot or pan, or write the letter which accompanied his five shilling postal order instead. Here

is the letter of thanks which I presented to Beaverbrook for his
signature : —

DEAR BABY KEITH WHITFIELD:

I send you my thanks for the money you have sent me.
I will use it to make the Air Force stronger so that it will
protect our homes.
And I admire the patriotic spirit which you have shown.
Yours sincerely,
Beaverbrook.

Simultaneously with the 'pots and pans' stunt came a similar
appeal for scrap metals. This was a more serious affair, carrying
mandatory overtones. Railings in squares and parks vanished
overnight; it was widely rumoured that it was on Beaverbrook's
insistence that his old enemy, Lord Baldwin, was compelled to
yield up the fine wrought-iron gates that guarded the entrance
to his Worcestershire mansion. It is probable that the call
'Bring us your scrap' did contribute in some slight measure to
the war effort. It is doubtful if the gifts of pots and pans created
a single new Spitfire or Hurricane, and as, a good deal later, this
fact seeped into the public's consciousness there arose an angry
murmur of complaint about Beaverbrook's showmanship. But
psychologically he had been right. To a considerable number of
people, mainly of the middle classes, he had given a sense of
purpose. In the period of agonized waiting for the invasion of
Britain which most of them now expected, they were given
the chance – so at the time they thought – of contributing something that would help their country to survive. The fact that
they might just as well have kept and used their pots and pans
was irrelevant. Later the sense of purpose for these citizens was
provided, during the blitz, by air-raid wardenship and fire-fight-
ing duties, but in those hot summer months when all Britain
held its breath, a letter from Beaverbrook thanking them for
'their invaluable services to the cause of freedom' (one of many
variants on the same theme in which I indulged) did mean
something.

The personal touch was equally, and perhaps more

effectively, in evidence in the Minister's attitude to the men actually employed in the aircraft industry. Directors or works managers of many small firms, sub-contractors for components needed for aircraft, who had never before had contact of any sort with the Government, were first alarmed, then flattered, finally enthused to hear a harsh, brash, Canadian accent asking them, direct from the Ministry or Stornoway House, to tell the Minister of their problems and shortages. Soon they found themselves bidden to telephone Beaverbrook personally every night at Stornoway House with the latest news of their output. Sometimes they were harshly criticized, more often they were told 'First rate' and went home to their semi-detached villas in the Midlands bursting with a pride which next morning they passed on to the men who worked for them. Often they would find, already pinned up in the works canteen, a telegram : 'To the workers at – – factory my warmest congratulations on a splendid output, Beaverbrook.' (It had usually been drafted by me at eleven o'clock at night, but in those early days had always been vetted by Beaverbrook before it was despatched.)

No one can prove statistically how much extra output these Beaverbrookian tactics achieved. They did, it is certain, create a sense of personal involvement in the nation's struggle. They complemented the oratory of Churchill, made it easier for the man at the lathe at Stoke-on-Trent, the housewife – pot and pan-less – queueing at Walton-on-Thames, really to believe it *was* their 'finest hour'.

Beaverbrook was a born play-actor, and in these days used this quality to its fullest bent. On the very day he was appointed Minister, the Society of British Aircraft Constructors was meeting in London. Suddenly the door was flung open and Beaverbrook entered the room. He spoke briefly. Urgency was his theme. This was not the moment for men in whose hands the fate of the country lay to be discussing their relations with each other, of all places in a committee room. Let them adjourn at once, go back to their factories and get down to it.

At Stornoway House the new Minister gave a party at which members of the new Government, and particularly Labour members, could meet and mingle with newspaper proprietors and correspondents from the Dominions and the United States. So far as the latter were concerned this was of real importance, for Beaverbrook well knew that his old friend (and only a year ago fellow-appeaser) the American Ambassador Joseph Kennedy, was telling them that Britain was finished. This particular drama however nearly turned into farcical tragedy. Among the Ministers present was that key figure in the Labour movement, the late Arthur Greenwood. Mr Greenwood, now one of the Big Five in the War Cabinet, like another key Labour figure a quarter of a century later, had one weakness, and when he yielded to it indiscretions followed thick and fast. Out of the corner of his eye Beaverbrook saw Greenwood, glass in hand, becoming extremely voluble. Swiftly I was detailed to cope with the situation. 'Get that damned fool Greenwood out of the house.' How I achieved this task I cannot now recall. I think I invented a telephone call to a non-existent War Cabinet meeting. Anyway I was able to usher the Lord Privy Seal to his waiting car. I regard the episode as one of my small contributions to the war effort.

Beaverbrook's critics have always maintained that he was little more than a play-actor and that his main object was self-glorification. The same criticism might also be levelled at the magnificent and flamboyant rhetoric to which at the same time Churchill was treating the House of Commons. Certainly the personal touch which the Minister of Aircraft Production used with high and low made him for a time the second most popular man in the country. It was rough magic worked with a nasal twang. It was effective as never quite again. In any case his critics were wrong. In all the six and a half years I worked for him I never knew him so selfless as in the months of his adopted country's greatest danger.

Nor could play-acting have got the results which were achieved. They came in the last resort from a rapid mastery, by the quickest and sharpest brain I have ever known, of all the problems and intricacies of the aircraft industry, allied to an incomparable drive. The final ingredient was a ruthlessness bordering sometimes on sharp practice which was perhaps natural in a man who had made a million before he was thirty, but which now was applied in the national interest. The 'personal touch' was the ingredient which fused these qualities into success.

Lord Salter (then Sir Arthur Salter) tells a story of Beaverbrook at his most ruthless and agile in those days. Salter was then Second Minister at the Ministry of Shipping, and they sat together in the ante-room at 10 Downing Street awaiting appointments with the Prime Minister. It was just after the fall of France, and from scraps of conversation from within Salter could tell that the argument was over what to do with a consignment of arms previously destined for the French. At length Churchill's visitor was ushered out – and Salter discovered that Beaverbrook had vanished. The Minister of Aircraft Production, who was not then even a member of the War Cabinet, was already on the telephone to the port where the consignment was held up. Before anyone quite knew what was happening it had become the property of MAP. How he got away with it Salter does not know. He suspects that Beaverbrook claimed the authority of the Prime Minister. It may not have been necessary. By this time, with MAP barely six weeks old, it was widely felt not only that it held the chief clue to success or failure in the battles that lay ahead, but that its Minister was Churchill's 'favourite son'.

For me, who in this doom-laden time of late spring and early summer saw him day in day out (including Sundays), and sometimes part of the night as well, the days had often the quality of a nightmare. The hasty scurryings between Stornoway House and Millbank, the increasing number of letters and documents for which I had to provide first drafts, the often brusque and always telegraphese instructions which had to be interpreted for onward transmission in the shortest form possible to the relevant individual or department, the absolute uncertainty as to what I was going to do next – all this put a strain on Beaverbrook's junior personal secretary that left its mark. Whenever I was not with him and my telephone rang I would jump in near panic out of my chair before I could bring myself to answer it. I had, after all, been catapulted into a strange alarming world for which nothing in my previous career had prepared me.

An even greater strain was placed on the senior personal secretary, George Malcolm Thomson. At that time and thereafter, he played a far more important role than I. I grew, I think, increasingly skilful at being 'His Master's Voice'. George was 'His Master's Ear'. He was his listening post, and where I observed, he gave advice which was listened to, and which on many occasions – though the Master never openly admitted it – caused a reversal of what Beaverbrook had originally intended.

It was a nightmare, but one in which, like other junior members of 'Operation Beaverbrook', I grew increasingly proud to share. For Beaverbrook it was a nightmare of a different kind, for if his nightmare turned into truth there would be a German occupation of Britain. This nightmare can be simply described. On the day he took office there were more trained pilots than there were aircraft in the front line of the RAF, and in Fighter Command there were only five fighter aircraft immediately available in reserve. The tensest, most nervous moment of the week was Saturday afternoon when Beaverbrook received the weekly production charts. From the start they rose steeply, and before the Battle of Britain was finally joined they showed a total reserve of sixty-five per cent of Fighter Command's operational strength, which at the same time exceeded the number of trained pilots available to man them. Such was the achievement which by every manner of means, adding up to inspired unorthodoxy, Beaverbrook had made possible. It came just and only just in time. In my view the Minister of Aircraft Production had his 'finest hour' even before Churchill had called upon the people of Britain to rise to theirs.

Beaverbrook maintained to me long afterwards that his most powerful and staunchest ally at this time was the man who would bear the brunt of the battle. The head of Fighter Command was Air Chief Marshal Sir Hugh Dowding. Later spiritualism was to take its toll of this dour, single-minded, humourless man, but at this time the fairies were still a long way from the bottom of his garden. He was in almost every way the opposite of Beaverbrook, but he believed in him and the belief was reciprocated. Dowding was tireless in telling everyone he could influence – in particular the 'Air Marshals' at the Air Ministry and the entourage at 10 Downing Street – that Beaverbrook must be deferred to in all things. Just before the fall of France, the French Premier, Paul Reynaud, sent an impassioned appeal that the remaining Fighter Squadrons of the RAF be sent to support the French army, already in full retreat. There was an urgent Cabinet meeting which Dowding attended. At first there looked like being a majority in favour, and Churchill the romantic, the lover of France, was at variance with Churchill the realist. I have no reason to disbelieve Beaverbrook's statement to me that it was his and Dowding's joint advocacy that swayed the Prime Minister against a decision which in the light of after events would have proved fatal. No squadrons were sent.

4

ENTER ALBERT NOCKELS

THOUGH WE had been forced to move to Millbank, right up to the night during the blitz when it was rendered uninhabitable by a German bomb Beaverbrook preferred to work at Stornoway House rather than at the Ministry. Not for nothing had his critics labelled him 'the Great Disorganizer', he revelled in this term of would-be opprobrium. The Minister's room at MAP was decorated with two slogans, which read 'Committees take the punch out of war' and 'Organization is the enemy of improvisation'. But slogans, he well knew, could not alter cases. An official Ministry spelled to him committees – committees in which the hated 'Air Marshals' through their MAP spokesman, Air Marshal Sir Wilfred Freeman, would have their impeding say. He hated committees anyway, they meant compromise and delay. The only kind for which he had any use was one over which he presided and which consisted of a small number of men guaranteed to agree with what he wanted to do. It was much easier to organize such gatherings at Stornoway House than on Millbank.

So, much of my time was spent in attendance, which meant in a top-floor bedroom, at Stornoway House, while Beaverbrook held discussions with kindred spirits from industry like Hennessy and Westbrook and, a little later, Hives, general manager of Rolls Royce, and Fedden, chief designer of the Bristol Aeroplane Company. It was at Stornoway House too that he would welcome groups of young RAF pilots, comrades of his son Max, and would discuss with them the performance of their aircraft, what they lacked and needed, where British planes were inferior to their German counterparts. To Beaverbrook these informal gatherings seemed far more useful than the elaborate programming that went on at his Ministry and at which, he had to admit, his civil servants were so devilish skilful.

It was at Stornoway House too that almost every evening about eight o'clock a mood of extreme, almost tangible tension would descend. On my way to a summons to the presence I would whisper to Albert, who frequently hung about in the hall: 'Has he telephoned yet?' and if Albert shook his head I would have to face something resembling a far from caged tiger. For it was at about this time that Max Aitken was due to telephone his father with news of that day's sortie over France, the Low Countries, or elsewhere. If the telephone failed to ring — but it always did, and immediately the tiger got back into his cage. Beaverbrook's elder son was a gallant and very skilled fighter pilot (he was shortly to be awarded the DFC — Distinguished Flying Cross); he also bore a charmed life. His father's admiration for him was unqualified, his devotion to him absolute.

For me personally, however, the most important event at this time was the arrival, sometime in that hot and pregnant summer, at Stornoway House of Albert Nockels. This remarkable character was to become during the next six years my constant companion, comforter and friend, the object of my affection, startled admiration, and, on occasions, astounded merriment.

Nockels arrived as newly-appointed valet to Lord Beaverbrook. The other Albert took his demotion very well. The new Albert never allowed anyone — his master included — to call him anything but Nockels. Therein lay the difference. The first Albert was essentially a humble man, constantly bullied by Beaverbrook and on the whole loving this treatment. Nockels was a very far from humble man, immensely conscious and jealous of his dignity. He was in fact a pedigree valet, and I have a suspicion, probably unfounded, that Beaverbrook may have chosen him in order to mark the change in his own status from newspaper proprietor to Cabinet Minister.

Nockels was tallish, balding, immaculately clad in short black coat and striped trousers, extremely impressive, with a voice that carried overtones of high society in almost every phrase. The nearest comparison I can give is with P. G. Wode-house's immortal Jeeves (though anything less like Bertie Wooster than Lord Beaverbrook it would be hard to imagine). But Jeeves was fiction, Nockels was very much a fact. His previous post had been with Princess Arthur of Connaught and he very soon made myself, and the rest of Beaverbrook's personal entourage, aware of the fact, and, in case we did not know, of Her Royal Highness's close relationship to the reigning monarch. One day much later in our joint career I remarked on the beauty of a pair of what looked like sapphire cuff-links. Indeed they *were* sapphire – Nockels would never have descended to imitation jewellery. 'Oh,' he said, 'do you like them? Princess Arthur gave them to me.' It was only one of many reminders he gave me from time to time of his semi-royal status. He gave Thomson another reminder. The latter had com-mented on a fine fur-lined coat which Nockels was wearing. 'Prince Arthur gave it to me.' The Prince had predeceased the Princess who inherited Nockels.

Nockels was equally impressive whether laying out his master's pyjamas or welcoming graciously, sometimes with a hint of condescension, the aircraft executives, civil servants, Cabinet Ministers, American visitors and others who came to call. Michael Foot has recently recalled one of the rare occasions on which he was worsted in such an encounter. Randolph Churchill appeared at Stornoway House, to be told by Nockels : 'The Lord is out walking.' 'On the water, I presume.' Nockels had no answer. It was never easy to answer the Prime Minister's irrepressible son.

Nockels was in fact nearly but not quite imperturbable. The chink in the armour of his imperturbability was his employer. The relationship between the two men was fascinating to watch. One wondered eagerly, yet apprehensively, how far each would go, Nockels with his air of a superior being immune to anything the man who by some mischance had the power to order him about might do to him; Beaverbrook with his recur-ring desire to humiliate this superior being in public. On the whole, during the next six years, Beaverbrook was perhaps the winner on points. On many occasions he broke through Nockels's defences by the vigour of his personality, and besides, Nockels grew increasingly admiring, as I did, of Beaverbrook's qualities, good *and* bad, and in either case outstanding. He could never have brought himself to resign. None the less Nockels had many victories too. One such occurred very early in their relationship. He and I were in a car with the Minister en route from Cherkley Court to the Ministry. The Battle of Britain was being waged. Our Spitfires and Hurricanes were chasing the Germans out of the sky – or so the BBC and the Press were somewhat mendaciously telling us. Beaverbrook was studying Cabinet papers. One of them flew out of the window. 'Stop stop,' Beaverbrook yelled. The car drew to a halt and Nockels prepared with unhurried mien to get out to retrieve the document. 'For God's sake, hurry up.' 'My Lord,' Nockels replied, 'I am not a Spitfire.'

As for Beaverbrook's feelings towards his new valet, they grew, I think, out of astonishment through irritation to real affection. Years later when, after I had left his employment, I was dining with him I told him some of the choicer Nockels stories of which he was unaware, in particular his welcome to General Eisenhower at Marrakesh.* He bellowed with warmhearted laughter. Nockels and I had at least one thing in common. In our different spheres we were each utterly unlike anyone Beaverbrook had employed before. It was perhaps to our credit that we learned, without totally losing our own identity, to swim the Beaverbrook way before we sank. But Nockels's was far the more self-confident, brisker breast stroke.

When Nockels joined Lord Beaverbrook the Battle of Britain had not yet begun. At about the same time another man was pressed into the Minister's service. Today such an appointment would be regarded as commonplace. Every important Minister appoints a high-powered public relations officer, drawn normally from the ranks of Fleet Street. But in 1940 the appoint-

* See page 125.

ment as MAP's director of publicity and propaganda of the News
Editor of the *Daily Express* caused many a raised Whitehall eye-
brow. What was the arch-priest of the unorthodox or (his
severer critics muttered) of self-advertisement up to now?
Among many other things he was up to the most publicized of
all his ballyhoos, the famous Spitfire Fund. It was the exploita-
tion of this fund which J. B. Wilson, who at sixty years of age
looked like a well-fed bishop and acted with a daemonic energy
highly uncharacteristic of the Church of England, was given as
his first task in his unexpected role of civil servant.

The fund needed no organization. It started indeed with a
gift from the people of Jamaica, sponsored by a local newspaper,
of a sum of money for the purchase of a bomber aircraft. But
Wilson and Beaverbrook were quick to see that it was not
bombers that would catch the imagination of the British public,
but fighters for their defence. So the Spitfire Fund it became, and
as such it snowballed rapidly to a total of a million pounds subscribed each month till Beaverbrook left MAP eleven months
later. In the mood of mingled Churchillian exaltation and more
down-to-earth apprehension in which Britain found itself, rais-
ing funds for Spitfires was money for jam. All Beaverbrook had
to do was to sign the letters of thanks which Thomson or I
wrote for him. All Wilson had to do was to ensure maximum
publicity for what he wrote. As with the pots and pans campaign the sums received were of no conceivable use for the
purpose for which they were subscribed. Certainly the Treasury
benefited, but money couldn't build Spitfires. It was men and
materials that were needed. To such a state of euphoria had
Beaverbrook reduced, or exalted, me that I was but dimly
aware of this as I wrote the letters of thanks. Perhaps for that
very reason they had a ring of sincerity. In any event, what
matter! It was all heady stuff and the public needed a taste of
champagne.

The Spitfire Fund was for Wilson a specific task. His general
brief was to ensure, by any and every means, maximum
publicity for MAP – and for its ministerial head. He succeeded
brilliantly, not only in Britain but in the Dominions and the
United States as well. The picture which Wilson, aided and

abetted by the cartoonist Low, drew of a human dynamo in
constant, peripatetic action made Beaverbrook the most talked
about man, apart from the Prime Minister, in the free world.
In many a mind at that time lay the unspoken question 'If
anything happened to Churchill. . . .' Beaverbrook did indeed
seem to many the most likely choice, and the idea was confirmed when he was appointed to the inner War Cabinet of
five. Herein lay the seeds of a bitter quarrel which was pro-
foundly to affect Beaverbrook's subsequent career. Waiting in
the wings, without benefit of publicity, was another potentially
very powerful candidate for the un-vacant seat. He was the
Minister of Labour, Ernest Bevin. The two men had already
clashed over the supply of manpower to the aircraft factories
and Churchill had come down on Beaverbrook's side. Bevin had
no use whatever for Beaverbrook's flamboyant publicity methods. This veteran Trade Union leader, commanding a greater
loyalty from Britain's working class than any other member of
Churchill's coalition cabinet, had one thing in common with
Beaverbrook. Both men had risen rapidly from obscurity to a
position of power. There the resemblance ended. Throughout
the war their mutual antipathy persisted. At this time Beaverbrook was riding high. Later it was to be different. The latter
did his best to wheedle Bevin into friendship. He would start a
letter 'My dear Ernie' and end 'Your devoted admirer, Max'. It
is doubtful whether Ernie was for an instant fooled.

The house that Max built was now nearly complete. Its solid
foundations were the Minister's Council, of which the outstanding members were Rowlands, Craven, Freeman and Hennessy.
Rowlands was the watchdog for the Civil Service, Freeman for
the Air Ministry. Craven and Hennessy, though civil servants
only by adoption, were quite capable of applying civil service
brakes to Beaverbrookian excesses and bad temper. To each of
these men Beaverbrook would listen, however impatiently
(though increasingly less to Freeman who later returned to the
Air Ministry). They provided the necessary minimum of
organization and level-headedness without which MAP would

have fallen apart. Of these four only Hennessy was Beaverbrook's own appointment. To them must perhaps be added
Colonel Llewellin, the Parliamentary Secretary, who, as the
Ministry's spokesman in the House of Commons, shielded
Beaverbrook from the many glancing blows delivered at him
even in the early days by mostly Conservative MPs. Peripheral
to this hard core were the men from industry, immune in
Beaverbrook's eyes from civil service inhibitions, whom he
brought in as a ginger group to get things done, often over the
heads of their superiors. These were his 'boys', eager to do his
bidding, uncritical of his commands. To this group, though he
became a member of the Minister's Council, Trevor Westbrook
in spirit belonged. MAP had in fact in many ways an anarchic
structure; it was always in danger of becoming a house divided
against itself. In due course this happened, and Beaverbrook
moved on. But in the summer and autumn of 1940 his method
of conducting his Ministry worked and it was exhilarating to
work in. In retrospect I am convinced that no more orthodox
structure could at that time and in that situation have achieved
nearly as much. By a hairsbreadth Beaverbrook and his lieu-
tenants produced just enough aircraft to ensure the country's
salvation.

One day in the early autumn of 1940 Beaverbrook was sent
by his Canadian friend, J. W. McConnell, a series of group photo-
graphs of young men in a weird assortment of clothing. 'They
don't look like angels,' he commented, 'but perhaps they can
fly.' They could and did. They were the first of the Canadian
volunteers collected by McConnell, who was proprietor of the
Montreal Star, to fly American aircraft across the Atlantic for
service with the RAF.

The decision to buy American planes was of course taken at
War Cabinet level, but it was Beaverbrook who in the organization of their purchase and transportation called in the men of
his native Canada, so that two of them at least became a sort of
superstructure to his Ministry. The more sober-sided was Morris
Wilson, President of the Royal Bank of Canada, an inter-

national figure, possessed of a grey quietness which concealed great drive and ability. Beaverbrook made him head of the new British Air Commission in New York. There was already in existence a British Purchasing Commission, but this organization was little to Beaverbrook's liking. It was all too apt to buy things for other Ministries.

Wilson would buy the planes, but who was to ferry them across the Atlantic? That was where the photographed young Canadians came in – and that was where J. P. Bickell came in too. For Beaverbrook set up yet another body, ATFERO (Atlantic Ferry Organization) and put his old friend Jack Bickell, whom he had known for forty years and who was now a director of International Nickel, at its head.

There was nothing grey about Jack Bickell. He wore loud suits, loud ties, loud hats. He smoked loud cigars, talked in wisecracks with a loud Canadian accent. At times he seemed to be playing the sheriff in a corny Western. To me – and to Nockels – he was a continual delight, a breath of overwhelming fresh air from the Canadian prairies (he was in fact city born and bred). Nockels used to gaze at him in wide-eyed astonishment, as at some exotic bird of paradise. He was one of the most overtly genial men I have ever met, and his geniality was certainly genuine.

How genuine were the claims that Beaverbrook made for him? Certainly ATFERO achieved remarkable results, but I have always suspected that they were due less to Bickell than to men like Captains Wilcockson and Bennett of the British Overseas Airways Corporation who trained the pilots, British, Dominion, American volunteers, who brought the planes over with the loss of only one aircraft in six months. But the claims were inevitable, for Bickell had for this fellow Canadian who had suddenly risen so much higher than he an unqualified, unquestioning admiration. Years later Bickell wrote to me about an article I had written, referring to 'Our Lord and Master' in terms that made it clear that he for one did believe that the Lord could walk on the water. To such an admirer Beaverbrook could not resist awarding unstinted praise.

In the wake of Jack Bickell came another Canadian R. B.

Bennett (soon to be made Lord Bennett for no discernible reason), an ex-Prime Minister of Canada. Apart from their devotion to Beaverbrook these men had little in common. Lord Bennett was an elderly, portly, genial, fatherly figure, to me graciously patronizing. I never knew quite what he was supposed to be doing. He settled down in a large mansion across the valley from Cherkley. He pottered about the Ministry, doing odd jobs. Sometimes he would preside over the opening of a new airfield, rather as if he was at a charity bazaar. It was, I am afraid, easy to see why his reign as Canadian Prime Minister had been so short. But he may have done the Ministry some good; he certainly did it no harm.

His influence, and that of Bickell, on the Minister is more debatable. Their praise of him, to his face and, he well knew, behind his back was fulsome and uncritical. They were powerful boosters of his ego, and the time was not far off when what he would need would be less praise and more measured criticism. The latter he could from a few people, and perhaps especially Sir Archibald Rowlands, take sometimes with reasonable grace, but the effect was apt to be spoiled by the heady praise of his pet cronies, among whom Bickell and Bennett were certainly numbered. The following dialogue is apocryphal, but it might easily have taken place.

The scene is Cherkley Court, late after dinner.

Beaverbrook	Jack, that fellow Rowlands won't let me commandeer that airfield for your fellows, without consulting the Cabinet.
Bickell	Say, Max, you're the boss, go ahead and do it.
Beaverbrook	Rowlands is a good man.
Bickell	He may be the best man on earth, but he's a civil servant.
Beaverbrook	How can I go against my chief advisers?
Bickell	Max, next to Churchill, *you're* the man the people trust.

There were too many well-meaning serpents – and not only Canadian serpents – in Beaverbrook's Garden of Eden.

So, as far as MAP was concerned, by early August the stage had been set, the chief actors assembled, for the high drama of the Battle of Britain and the Blitz. There had been minor dramas already, with happy endings and Beaverbrook taking all the bows while distributing bouquets to all around him. And there had been comedies too, in one of which *in absentia* I took part. Beaverbrook had instituted a rule whereby letters written for his signature by Thomson had to have a small 't' in the top right hand corner, those written by me a small 'f'. One evening about half past eight, with his full Council surrounding him, Beaverbrook pressed the bell which summoned me to his presence. I had gone home, so Thomson, with an air of conscious virtue, answered the summons. Beaverbrook looked up as he entered the room. 'Where's little f?' 'Little f,' replied Thomson, 'has effed off.'

In the ensuing gale of laughter at this unexpected sally, my truancy was forgotten. It was a very human Ministry to work in, led by a very human man.

5

THE BATTLE AND THE BLITZ

THE BATTLE OF BRITAIN has been written about and mulled over in many books; it is commemorated annually in the air and in the churches. It lasted from early August to mid-September 1940. The victory, magnificent in any case, was at the time wildly exaggerated in terms of German aircraft brought down, but the figure given of 185 destroyed on 15 September was a boost to public morale just when it was to be put to its severest test. The victory was shown, once the dust had settled, to have lain not in the fact that the Luftwaffe had been badly mauled but that Fighter Command by the narrowest of margins had survived.

Churchill later stated: 'Lord Beaverbrook was at his very best when things were at their very worst.' From personal observation I can confirm this verdict. He was at this time an inspiration to those who worked for him, though at times he drove them ragged with his demands. On one occasion during the battle he drove *me* ragged. Thomson had warned me at the start of my new career that if, when the need arose, I did *not* have a stand-up fight with my employer, I would be a lost soul. Early one morning Beaverbrook summoned me to his room at the Ministry and gave me instructions for three memoranda on differing subjects. I had then been working every day without a break for three months. Some forty minutes later my bell rang. In full view of his Council the Minister turned on me. 'God damn it, where are those memoranda?' Something in me snapped. 'How the hell do you expect me to do three things all at once in half an hour?' I shouted, turned on my heel, slammed the door and was gone.

Back in the secretaries' room, still seething, I awaited my

doom. Unknown to me, on the other side of the door Sir Charles Craven was saying: 'Max, if you want to keep that young man you'd better give him a day off, and pretty quick.' Thereafter Thomson and I had every other Sunday free.

Beaverbrook never mentioned the incident to me. In a sense I had won a little battle of my own. Imperceptibly the relation between us changed from that of master and servant to that of employer and employee. On occasions my advice was asked, in the sense that he would make a statement and dare me to challenge it. Through a purely fortuitous loss of temper I had established myself in his eyes as a person in my own right.

Unknown to me till shortly afterwards I had an unsolicited ally in my campaign against continuous Sunday working. Grannie Mackett wrote to the Minister of Aircraft Production as follows:

You are doing what you believe to be best for your country. Does God think so? Remember to keep Holy the Sabbath Day still counts. Excuses won't profit us, they only make worse the offence. I am referring to Sunday munition work and Sunday pleasure. As far back as 1895 England was warned of sin and since and in 1913 our Saviour God was so troubled about us all that He came three times in Person to save souls. Did people believe or care, very few and those who enquired were lied to. He not only commanded me to tell others of His coming here, but allowed a clergyman to overlook my brain to see His messages and to save time and mistakes. The King has commanded Sunday 26 May as a Day of Prayer. The Greater King more so, but can he bless war instruments made upon His Day of Rest. Sin is the cause of war, what right have we to judge Hitler, though we all think of him as an evil man. Do not believe what I write, but ask God like Gideon of old for a sign (Judges 6) that England is wrong and also ask the Archbishop of Canterbury and also Canon Warner at Eastbourne, whom God allowed to see His Messages.

> I am, Yours truly,
> Grannie E. Mackett.

Meanwhile battle turned into blitz. For a week the two over-lapped. The victory of Fighter Command occurred on Sunday 15 September, the first great bomber raid occurred on London's dockland in broad daylight eight days earlier. Thomson and I, who were working in the Ministry, had from our sixth floor windows a grandstand view of the awesome spectacle. In beautiful formation, unmolested by British fighters, the German bombers flew towards us up the Thames, then, a bare two hundred yards from us, turned to make their run. Amid the crash of anti-aircraft fire the bombs began to fall. Soon great billows of smoke began to rise, turning green to sultry yellow as the oil installations caught fire. The sky over dockland became obscured, and through the murk could be seen the leaping, all-devouring flames. It looked like total destruction. It was the only time when I personally thought that the war would be lost.

George Malcolm Thomson and I were undoubted witnesses to this terrifying spectacle. So according to the other book I wrote about him,* was Beaverbrook himself. I spent many weary hours, abetted by Thomson, in trying to persuade him to the contrary, for his personal secretaries had with their own eyes seen him depart for Cherkley immediately after lunch, and the raid had not started till after three. To no avail. It was, I think, inconceivable to him in retrospect that he, the Minister of Aircraft Production, should not have been witness to this cataclysmic moment in air warfare; so he was there – and that was all there was to it. Weakly I yielded; after all, the book could not be written without his assistance and inspiration.

He *was* there almost before the raid was over. As soon as he got news of it he rushed back to London, summoned his Council and that evening took the vital decision to commandeer, on his own responsibility, every inch of factory space all over the country not at present in use, so that the aircraft industry could be dispersed. This decision, taken without consultation, enraged many of his Government colleagues. It damaged the country's overall production, it delayed, his critics were to say, the hour of final victory. But it saved the day. Few realized at

* *The Sky's The Limit*, London, 1943.

the time how nearly the Blitz destroyed both the will and the ability of Britain to fight on; and the ability meant then the production of aircraft. During all the months of the Blitz that production continued to rise.

The day of 7 September had for me a startling postscript. Emerging from the Ministry after the raid was over I went to dine with a friend in South Kensington. In a state of horrified over-excitement I started to tell him what I had seen. I was met by an air of scepticism bordering on incredulity. I had forgotten what a far cry dockland was from Onslow Square. He had not even heard the raid. All was quiet while we dined, and I recovered a measure of my composure. At about ten o'clock I prepared to leave. My host opened the door. As I stepped onto the pavement there was an enormous explosion as a bomb, heralding the night Blitz, fell across the Square. I bolted back inside. At last my friend believed. I stayed the night.

The attack on dockland was the only major daylight air raid, but many minor ones were to follow. Air raids meant air-raid warnings, which in turn, by Cabinet decision, meant mandatory descent to air-raid shelters, which meant to Beaverbrook delays in production. At any rate, so far as MAP was concerned, it took at least five minutes for the Minister and his entourage to descend from the sixth floor to the basement; the bomb was likely to catch them half way down. Soon Beaverbrook was breaking the rule, as were some of his Council and perforce his secretaries. One felt curiously exposed as a part of London's skyline; sometimes we could see the bomber approaching. One afternoon the sirens sounded. Thomson and I bent ourselves with what application we could to the tasks in hand. Then came the dreaded whine. Simultaneously we plunged beneath the table, our heads colliding. The bomb fell harmlessly into the Thames. Shakily we emerged and sat again at the big desk we then shared. Scarcely had we done so when Beaverbrook burst into the room. 'Good boys,' he cried, seeing us apparently unruffled and at work. 'Good boys. That's the way to show 'em.'

Man-hours lost in the factories through air-raid warnings became with Beaverbrook an obsession. He stormed and raged against the system, demanding in vain in Cabinet that air-raid warnings be abolished altogether, apparently unaware that for every aircraft worker who was a super-patriot there were at least ten who preferred an air-raid warning as a chance to save their skins. He did indeed persuade himself that the aircraft workers were a sort of special corps d'élite under his personal command. It was a sign both of his strength and his weakness, of his utter absorption in this immediate task to the increasing exclusion of wider considerations. He employed Admiral Sir Edwards Evans* to tour his factories, boosting morale, but was later to find that the dashing ex-sailor's rumbustious methods of exhortation were by no means to all his audience's taste. He visited every stricken area himself. I can remember him setting forth early in the morning after the raid on Coventry, and returning, worn and grey-faced, late that evening. With him he brought William Rootes, the city's biggest industrialist. That night he put Rootes in charge of the Coventry Reconstruction Committee. He had no time – perhaps no inclination – for consultation with other Ministers, but the Committee acted for all the Ministries concerned in war production, Beaverbrook's factories getting, of course, first priority. Within a few weeks the Committee had created order out of complete chaos, and production had been more than half restored.

It was the same with Birmingham, Southampton, Merseyside. Beaverbrook in those months rode the whirlwind as, I think, no other single Minister, and certainly no Cabinet Committee could have. But the personal touch was taking a heavy physical and mental toll. Physically asthma began to rear its ugly head. Mentally he grew increasingly resentful of the slightest opposition to the series of improvisations which were his idea of planning, and especially of opposition, however often overridden, in Cabinet. He had the almost constant support of Churchill, the increasing opposition of Ernest Bevin. During the

* Famous in World War I as 'Evans of the Broke', the hero of Zeebrugge.

Blitz it was Beaverbrook who normally gained the day. His needs were so obviously paramount. But other Ministers watched in some alarm as the Prime Minister walked the tight-rope between these two born antagonists.

Beaverbrook had, by the time of the Coventry raid, been in office for six months. He could on occasion charm the hind leg off a donkey. In the early days he had used his immense charm to get what he wanted from other ministers, some of whom he had previously assailed in his newspapers. In particular, one summer morning he charmed the then Secretary of State of War, Anthony Eden. I remember Eden passing through the private office with a worried and determined frown on his face. Half an hour later Beaverbrook was ushering him out. 'Fine, Anthony, fine. You're a great Minister'; and Eden's face was wreathed in smiles. Later we learned that Beaverbrook had got about ninety per cent of what he wanted. But in the last months of 1940 the charm was wearing thin. His shock tactics too were incurring increasing opposition from other Ministers who, believing rightly that the Blitz was failing, were seeking to plan further ahead. For all his power to charm Beaverbrook was, as he once told me, 'a cat that walks alone'. His miaows of protest to the Prime Minister grew steadily in volume. It was about this time that the stream of resignation letters began.

Thomson and I counted fourteen of these letters despatched to 10 Downing Street before Beaverbrook resigned from the Government in February 1942. Later one of Churchill's private secretaries added a fifteenth of which we had been unaware, written in Beaverbrook's own hand. In the midst of this stream one of the typists in the private office decided to resign. I drafted for her a mock letter of resignation which read as follows: –

My DEAR MAX,

I have been thinking over our conversation of last night. But it is not possible for me to remain at your service in the Government.

My task is finished, and it is necessary that I should now hand it over to my successor. If my health and temper would permit I would gladly continue to serve under your banner.

But my asthma is a constant trouble to me. I am not able to see things clearly in the mornings, and sometimes I see even less clearly after dinner.

For some time now I have been uncomfortable in my position. I am in constant disagreement with my colleagues. And it will be better that you should no longer be troubled with these issues which lead only to bad feeling and delays. But in laying down my burden at this stage I take pride in having played a part in the glorious achievements of the past year of which you have been the sole and splendid architect.

And in the years to come it will be a source of joy to me that you chose me as a helper in the great fight for freedom, democracy, and the development rights of Cherkley.*

Your devoted servant,

Barbara.

It was parody, of course, but it was not too far from the originals. They followed an identical pattern. 'I must lay down my burden' – 'You have sustained me in my times of trial and tribulation' (the biblical touch which he used so often) – 'I have been proud to serve under your banner' (this was certainly genuine; Beaverbrook was at heart a deeply sentimental man, and his devotion to Churchill was at this time complete) – a reference to 'my asthma' as an inhibiting factor – 'My task is finished, another can now better shoulder the tasks ahead.'

Did Beaverbrook mean these letters of resignation to be accepted? I do not think he knew himself. Partly they were induced by frustration – they usually followed a Cabinet refusal of something he wanted. Partly they were due to the not un-justified feeling that, as the second most important man in the country (or so Bickell, Bennett and other cronies told him), he was entitled to his own way. They carried an implied threat, 'Gimme, or else – – ' Partly they were a reaction to the way he drove himself, showing a real desire for a little peace and quiet, and perhaps a bit of sniping from the sidelines. Certainly they

* Beaverbrook was at the time bitterly opposing in the Cabinet a proposal to limit the powers of landlords to make money out of the development of their properties.

did not help to ease the burdens under which the Prime Minister laboured; nor was Beaverbrook usually slow to accept Churchill's refusal to countenance them.

In one recurring phrase anyway there was a good measure of truth – 'Another man now can better shoulder the tasks ahead.' By the end of 1940 the Blitz was dying down, only to be briefly revived with land-mine attacks in April 1941. It was becoming increasingly obvious that Britain would not lose the war, the problem was how to win it. It could not be solved by short-term measures, by the methods by which Beaverbrook had averted defeat. The need was for long-term planning, of which the incumbent Minister of Aircraft Production had little experience and for which he had no liking. Moreover the war could not be won in the air alone. There was need for tanks, for guns, for merchant ships. The War Office, the Ministry of Shipping would have to be given priorities, and without top priorities, Churchill well knew, Beaverbrook would soon be sulking in his tent. And so, in April 1941 one of the resignation letters was, with qualifications, accepted. Beaverbrook should leave MAP, but he would remain in the War Cabinet with the vague title of Minister of State and equally vague supervisory duties over every aspect of production. It was, on the face of it, a ridiculous appointment, for whatever else he was Beaverbrook was ill-cast as a supervisor; and in fact the appointment lasted exactly a fortnight. But Churchill needed his friend in the Cabinet and in the last resort Beaverbrook was not at that time – perhaps at no time – prepared to deny him. With, in private to his personal secretaries, much wailing and gnashing of teeth, he accepted the post.

It was at this time that I fell temporarily by the wayside. I wrote to my master telling him regretfully that I was laid low by an attack of water on the knee. To my letter I received the following reply :

DEAR FARRER,

I am so sorry that you have water on the knee.
I am just as sorry to say that I have water on the eye.
And I hope that you will soon be well enough to come

back and help poor Thomson who cannot keep *his* water in the proper place.*

Yours sincerely,
Beaverbrook.

To such a man a great deal, so far as I was concerned, could be forgiven.

So we moved into 12 Downing Street. A splendid, reverberating address of which I made fullest use in conversation with my friends. A door that led straight through to No. 10, an unimpeded view of No. 10's garden where the great man would pace, in boiler suit, in consultation with a colleague or, in rare moments of relaxation, with Mrs Churchill. It was even possible on occasions, for the secretaries to eavesdrop. It seemed a sad comedown when our next port of call proved to be Shell-Mex House in the Strand. It wasn't.

---

* This was, of course, a gross libel. Thomson generously refrained from suing.

6

MINISTER OF SUPPLY

TOWARDS THE end of May the Beaverbrook caravan folded their tents and moved on. Shell-Mex House was the headquarters of the Ministry of Supply, and with the by now customary protestations and complainings, Beaverbrook accepted this fresh post. Churchill had, I believe, earmarked it for him some time previously. He could not seriously have believed that the Dictator at MAP could suddenly become a success as a co-ordinating, conciliating Minister of State. Anyway it was a shrewd appointment.

The caravan consisted of Beaverbrook, Thomson, Farrer – and Nockels. We were the sole survivors from MAP. Left behind, alas! were Rowlands – in my mind then and in his later, even more distinguished posts, one of the great civil servants of all time – Hennessy, John Eaton Griffiths, and many others who had bestowed on that odd fish, Beaverbrook's junior personal secretary, the gift of their friendships. At Shell-Mex House we had to start all over again. Edmund Compton had preceded us there, but was apart from the Minister's private office.

Almost imperceptibly Nockels the valet was becoming Nockels the friend and confidant. Long ago, almost from the start, he had reached that position with me, now he was spreading the net of his remarkable personality far and wide. To his actual employer he was, as was only right and proper, suitably deferential. It was 'Good morning, Sir,' 'The car is waiting, Sir,' and, the Spitfire incident excluded, a dignified haste in ministering to Sir's needs. (His private comments to me were sometimes less decorous.) But to others, high or low, who came within Beaverbrook's orbit, he was increasingly hail fellow, well met. 'Hullo, Sir, how are you.' He was particularly successful with the Americans who in growing numbers were visiting Beaverbrook at MAP and then the Ministry of Supply, or on Sundays at Cherkley, for Beaverbrook had given up the unequal struggle to make his civil servants work a seven-day week. To these visitors Nockels was a sheer delight, the epitome of what they had always imagined an English gentleman's gentleman to be. Did they sense that he might have been more at home, though he would have had far less fun, at Chatsworth than at Cherkley? No matter, there he was, perhaps a little larger than life, courteous, dignified, welcoming, a gentleman's gentleman, but, he gently implied, a gentleman himself as well. I think he felt an innate English superiority in their presence, but he never showed it. He was graciously pleased to greet them as equals – hiding his deep sense of shock at the sight of Harry Hopkins's clothes – and they loved it.

Of these visiting Americans, three remain vividly in my memory. Harry Hopkins and Averell Harriman were harbingers of aid and comfort sent by President Roosevelt at a time when he could do little more. Each played an outstanding role in bringing about Lend-Lease, the first concrete step America took to buttress Britain's resistance. John G. Winant was Roosevelt's accredited representative as Ambassador at the Court of St James's.

Harry Hopkins first appeared in London during the Blitz. He was as unobtrusive a man as I have ever known. He would enter the Secretaries' office so quietly that sometimes one was unaware that he was there, waiting to see the Minister. Then one would look up to see a slight, almost waif-like looking man, clad in shabby raincoat and battered trilby. He would go in to see Beaverbrook. A little later I would perhaps be summoned. Hopkins would be sunk, almost invisible, in an armchair somewhere in the corner of the room. Seldom can a man's appearance have so belied his character. Hopkins was already a sick man,* but the flame within burned fiercely. A passionate advocate of and believer in Britain, he had a mind that was razor sharp, a delight in the seemingly impossible that matched Beaverbrook's

* He died in the decade after the war.

own, and the complete confidence then, and throughout the war, of his President. He was in fact the Crown Prince who could never become King. The same confidence was awarded him by Churchill and Beaverbrook. Later he and the Prime Minister were to cross swords, at Yalta and elsewhere, as British and American ideas of the world's future began to conflict. But while Britain stood alone under a hail of bombs Hopkins was the strongest buttress of Roosevelt's belief in our survival.

It is hard to imagine a greater outward contrast than Averell Harriman. He looked indeed the *beau idéal* of a British rather than an American diplomat. He was dark and very handsome with sleek black hair immaculately brushed and clothes that satisfied Nockels's most exacting standards. Though he was by profession an industrialist who had become President of the Union Pacific Railroad and had been pressed into Government service by Roosevelt, he was by temperament more of a diplomat than Hopkins. At first he played second fiddle, but Roosevelt could not spare the latter long from his side. Hopkins's visits to England were flying ones. It was Harriman whom the President established as his permanent representative in London and Harriman who was the more frequent visitor throughout the war to Cherkley. He was *persona grata* in Government and many other circles; he became a superb interpreter of the British point of view.

Perhaps I am prejudiced. On one occasion, flying the Atlantic, Harriman noticed me just finishing a new book by Walter Lippman. He asked me to tell him about it. To the best of my ability I did so. At this moment Beaverbrook came down the aisle. 'Max,' said Harriman, 'you've got a brilliant young man here. He's just told me in five minutes all I want to know about a book it would have taken me three hours to read.' Beaverbrook was not *altogether* pleased. But my wartime admiration for Harriman has been justified by events. Many now consider that he has proved the ablest of all post-war diplomats. At the time of writing, in his late seventies, he is still hard at it.

If Hopkins and Harriman looked and in many respects were unalike, John G. Winant was unlike them both. He represented, in the Embassy at Grosvenor Square, a pinnacle after an abyss.

He succeeded Joseph Kennedy, father of the future president, and one of the most unpopular ambassadors of all time, and he won from the British public a respect and admiration seldom paralleled. I saw far less of him than of Hopkins or Harriman, for he saw far less of Beaverbrook. The two men were in many respects incompatibles. Winant exuded integrity; Beaverbrook, though he possessed it, seemed often by his manner and sometimes his actions to deny its possession. Winant was reserved and shy, Beaverbrook was extrovertly exuberant. Winant by his writings has shown himself imbued with a deep religious sense, Beaverbrook, though he boasted of his Presbyterian ancestry, though he was much addicted to biblical quotation, though on occasions he would startle dinner guests by bidding Nockels put the hundredth psalm on the gramophone, was not in the accepted sense a religious man. Again, you could not by any stretch of imagination cast Beaverbrook in the role of Abraham Lincoln, Winant not only looked but acted the part. In fairness to both men, there was far less need for direct contact between them than between Beaverbrook and the other two. Winant had no direct concern with the supply of materials.

When Beaverbrook moved to the Ministry of Supply the war was in the doldrums. The fierce gales of 1940 had ceased to blow. 'Sail on O Ship of State,' Roosevelt had cabled to Churchill at the height of the storm, and at least the ship of state had remained afloat. But as yet, there was no favouring wind, and from one quarter a new gale was likely to threaten. It was the Middle East. Here in the Western Desert a game of see-saw was in progress – people were said to be wagering in Cairo on whether the British or the Axis forces would get to Benghazi *and back* in the faster time. In the early summer of 1941, due largely to Britain's unsuccessful attempt to prevent the over-running of Greece, the advantage lay heavily with the Axis. Tobruk was invested, the British were back inside the borders of Egypt. It was said that we were inferior in armour and above all in tanks. Here was a new priority; for aircraft read tanks, for Beaverbrook read Beaverbrook.

There was a difference however between May 1940 and May 1941. In 1940 Beaverbrook had built up a new Ministry almost from scratch, and was himself a new phenomenon. Moreover, Churchill, the unchallenged leader, had been in a position to give his friend *carte blanche*. In 1941 Beaverbrook took over a Ministry in complete running order and fully staffed. He had too, as he was always the first to admit, made in the intervening year many and powerful enemies – his methods made this inevitable – whose enmity the mantle of Churchill could no longer cloak. His power of action was for the first time circumscribed. There was another difference. Beaverbrook had never been seriously criticized for the sort of aircraft he produced. In his later days as Minister of Supply he was vigorously assailed for producing the wrong kind of tanks. In particular, the brilliant Western Desert correspondent of his own *Daily Express*, Alan Morehead, was forthright in his criticisms in his despatches. On his return to London Beaverbrook sent for him to Cherkley, argued with him, pleaded with him. Morehead remained adamant.

I never felt the same sense of high purpose, almost of exaltation at Shell-Mex House as I had at MAP. The Ministry of Supply was filled with men of great ability. Harold Macmillan, the Parliamentary Secretary, was an abler and far more ambitious man than Llewellin. Sir William Brown, the Permanent Secretary, lacked Rowlands's force of character and was too much a civil servant ever to win Beaverbrook's complete confidence or friendship; but the fault was not his, and he was widely respected for his abilities and his loyalty to his staff. The private secretaries, Pearson and Robert (Robbie) Burns, were as friendly as Eaton Griffiths and Compton, and as ready, once they got used to him, to share a joke about the Minister behind his back. But somehow, for me, things weren't what they used to be. Perhaps it was because my devotion, this side idolatry, for Beaverbrook in the great days of 1940 had been modified into high but sometimes critical admiration.

In the early morning of 22 June 1941 Hitler launched his attack on Russia, and in the evening Churchill made his famous speech, welcoming the Russians with open arms. Subsequently three men maintained that they were the first to reach the Prime Minister at Chequers and advise him on the course to take. Anthony Eden, Sir Stafford Cripps (on leave from the Embassy at Moscow) and Beaverbrook all staked their claim. I only know that directly my telephone call (see Chapter 2) had given him his first hard news Beaverbrook set off by car from Cherkley. But the question who got there first is totally irrelevant. The whole Cabinet had known for weeks that the attack was pending and had decided on what line to take. It is clear now that the only man in the world who refused to believe it was coming was Joseph Stalin. He had set his heart on appeasement, in that alone resembling Neville Chamberlain.

The invasion of Russia proved decisive in the defeat of Germany. But for the moment all the British could do was to witness the Russians reeling back towards the very outskirts of Moscow and Leningrad. There could be no thought of diversionary measures, the idea of a Second Front had not even entered Beaverbrook's head. There were neither the men nor the weapons. It was the task of the Minister of Supply to provide the latter. He set his targets high, careless again of the demands of other Ministries. Another man might have aimed lower and hit his target. It was better Beaverbrook's way, even though old frictions grew more dangerous.

A surprising by-product of the invasion of Russia was Beaverbrook's induction into the field of international conferences. But before his famous Mission to Moscow came the Atlantic Charter. Beaverbrook was not of the party which early in August boarded HMS Prince of Wales at Scapa Flow to sail to meet President Roosevelt at Placentia Bay, Newfoundland. But even while he was still at sea Churchill sent him a message asking him to fly out to join him. In Churchill's own words: 'Before starting on my voyage I thought it would be best for Lord Beaverbrook to deal for us with the whole question of American supplies to Russia.'* Why he did not take his friend

* *Their Finest Hour* (Vol. II of *The Second World War*), London and Boston, 1949.

with him on the voyage has never been explained. He summoned Arthur Purvis, head of the British Purchasing Commission, at
the same time. The two men flew on separate aircraft. It was
Purvis's that crashed, killing everyone on board.

At Placentia Bay Beaverbrook argued hotly on the vexed
question of Article IV of the proposed joint declaration by
President and Prime Minister, which dealt with the post-war
access 'on equal terms' by all nations to the trade and raw
materials of the world. He succeeded in getting this clause modified in a manner that would enable him, when peace came, to
mount again his favourite hobby horse of Empire Free Trade.
Then, while Churchill sailed home, he proceeded to Washington to indulge in discussions that were the curtain raiser to the
journey to Moscow which the Prime Minister had now planned
for him. Six weeks later he was off.

Almost from the day of the German invasion Stalin had been
bombarding Churchill with angry telegrams demanding diversionary action in the West, twenty British divisions to be sent
either to Archangel or through neutral Persia to the Caucasus,
a landing on the coast of France. The Prime Minister's answer
was to send Beaverbrook, with a high ranking mission and
Averell Harriman representing the now committed but still non-
belligerent United States, to beard the devious dictator in his
own den and to offer him largely increased supplies of aircraft,
tanks and other war material. It was a perilous journey, from
Scapa Flow to Archangel, with Nockels enduring agonies of
sea-sickness as the cruiser pitched and rolled its way round the
North Cape and Thomson giving his fretsome master what
cheer and comfort he could: it was the prelude to one of
Beaverbrook's more spectacular wartime successes. He gave me
his own, uninhibited version of what had happened after his
return to London.

He had in fact succeeded in charming the uncharmable. The
sullen Dictator in the Kremlin had yielded to his blandishments
to an extent that not even Roosevelt, much less Churchill, ever
achieved. With the invaluable Harriman at his side, he praised

and he promised, praised the gallantry of the great Russian armies, promised in specific terms – so many aircraft, so many tanks each month. There was haggling, but less than he had feared. It became obvious that he was promising more than Stalin expected. He was also promising in excess of his London brief, but for the moment the weather, in Moscow at least, was set fair. 'God damn it, Farrer,' he said, 'we spent more time eating and drinking than sitting round the conference table.' The final banquet was a sore trial to his liver. There was no escaping as toast followed endless toast. It was hard to recall that the Germans were almost at the gates. Beaverbrook noticed that for every toast a special glass was provided from which Stalin could drink. He felt that he was in Borgia country. There was rough and ready conversation. 'Tell me,' asked Beaverbrook, 'does Kalinin [the Russian President] have a mistress?' 'No, he's far too old. Do you?' Stalin must have marked the contrast between the dynamic, effervescent man who sat beside him and the left-wing intellectual whom Britain had early in 1940 ill-advisedly sent him as her ambassador. It would have been far better to have sent a duke or, better still, a member of the Royal Family. It would have been easier to understand a Tory than a man who thought he understood Russian communism. Sir Stafford Cripps in fact took little part in these Moscow discussions. He had hurried back from Kuibishev, to which the diplomatic corps had been evacuated. Stalin parted with Beaverbrook on friendly terms. For a long while the latter was the only leading Englishman he trusted. More than a year later he was asking for him as ambassador in Moscow.

Beaverbrook's mission brought concrete aid to Russia when she sorely needed it; it was also a morale-booster for the sorely tried Russian people. It brought to Britain temporary relief from the demand for action in the West. It had been a success, but if Beaverbrook expected to return in triumph he found that it was to be short-lived. Soon the hornets were about his ears.

Their nests were mainly in the War Office and the Air Ministry. The latest British dash for Benghazi was petering out. The cry was for more tanks and just at this moment it was discovered that, though the Ministry of Supply were providing tanks in bountiful numbers, the spare parts to go with them were the wrong shape and size. The cry was for more aircraft too and Beaverbrook was busily shipping both these weapons of war to the Russians in much greater numbers than had originally been intended. For the first time it was being openly whispered that the man was impossible to work with. In his own Ministry he never inspired the devotion which had been his at MAP. It was about this time that the Parliamentary Secretary, Harold Macmillan, told Harold Nicolson that 'Beaverbrook gave no man his complete confidence.'* The criticism was justified. When he was absent, at Placentia Bay, in Moscow and later in Washington, he was careful to leave divided responsibility in his Ministry behind him. Macmillan and Sir William Brown, the Permanent Secretary, both, I think, felt that on his return Beaverbrook would ask each how the other had been getting on. It may have been the feeling that he might even ask his junior personal secretary that prompted Macmillan on one occasion when Beaverbrook was away to ask me out for a drink. It was the first time that I had ever spoken to him.

Faced on his return from Moscow with these unexpected difficulties and criticisms, Beaverbrook was at his most irascible. There were at least two letters of resignation, and the members of his caravan suffered. Nockels was harried mercilessly, I came under constant criticism, only Thomson, the wise counsellor, seemed immune. Beaverbrook throughout his ministerial career oscillated wildly between a feeling that he was indispensable and that he must get out. It was frequently when he felt the former that he announced to his friends his determination to do the latter, but in those post-Moscow days, stung by the criticisms of him that had so suddenly come to light, he really felt that he should go. For a man who had made himself a millionaire and built himself a newspaper empire he had a remarkably thin political skin.

* *Harold Nicolson, Diaries and Letters, 1939-45*, London and New York, 1967.

Then came Pearl Harbour, and forty-eight hours later what seemed then, and still seems to me now, the incredible German declaration of war on the United States. I remember my own overwhelming feeling when I heard the news of the latter event in a Soho pub. I had, with Beaverbrook in the Government, known a good deal more of the inside story of the war than the general public, and rather more, through unauthorized perusal of Cabinet documents, than perhaps I should. Time and again during the previous six months I had asked myself, and asked Thomson: 'How the hell are we going to *win*?' There seemed no possible answer. Churchill might have declaimed earlier: 'Give us the tools and we will finish the job,' but wars cannot be won by tools alone. What was needed was manpower. Now at last it would be forthcoming in limitless measure. Hitler had done for us what even Roosevelt had been unable to perform.

Churchill was quick to act. Within hours he had arranged a grand conference in Washington to plan allied strategy and had asked Beaverbrook to accompany him to talk about production. For once Beaverbrook did not play hard to get. Within a week the Argosy departed from the mouth of the River Clyde in search of the Golden Fleece that was American manpower and supplies.

George Malcolm Thomson has brilliantly and fully described in his book *Vote of Censure** the events and results of this conference, including my own temporary disturbance of Churchill's peace of mind when he read a cable of mine to Beaverbrook underlining press criticism of the great man. This criticism, centring on the rapid deterioration of our position in the Far East, was being voiced alike from the Right and Left. 'Who is this fellow Farrer?' Churchill remarked. It is the only time a Prime Minister has ever referred to me in person.

It is Thomson's view that Beaverbrook in Washington performed a task second in importance only to his direction of MAP in the summer of 1940. His aim was simply to persuade the United States Government to double its existing production

* London, New York, 1968, chapters 1 and 3.

targets. He knew the Americans better than any other member of the British Mission and he had the complete confidence of Roosevelt and Hopkins. He went to work on the big industrialists who were in charge of war production. He appealed to them with a mixture of passion and cunning. He played on the American desire to emulate and excel. 'Anything you can do I can do better' was soon to be the hit song in a famous American musical. Anticipating the song's title and reversing it, he sang to them 'Anything *I* can do *you* can do better.' Annie Get Your Gun! The Americans reached for it at once. The sights were raised, and in the event almost all the targets were reached.

The Mission returned to England well satisfied with itself. The main objectives had been achieved; above all Churchill had persuaded Roosevelt to make the war in Europe his first priority. It received when it got home a welcome that varied from chilly to frozen. Nothing could have surprised or angered Churchill more. Basking in the warmth of his American reception he had seemed careless of the disasters that were happening on the other side of the world and certainly unaware of their effect on public opinion as chronicled by 'that fellow Farrer' in his telegrams to Beaverbrook. I like to think that the latter did pay some heed to them, and had some inkling of the storms ahead. His mood when he returned indicated as much. 'My asthma' was a recurring theme in his conversation and 'my asthma' usually meant more letters of resignation. Nockels, who of course saw him in his most unguarded early morning moments, gave me his weather report which added up to 'showers, few bright intervals, violent thunderstorms imminent'.

The loss of the Prince of Wales and Repulse, the pride of Britain's Navy, the rapid Japanese advance down the Malayan Peninsula, the loss of the Philippines, the threat to Singapore and indeed to the whole of the Dutch East Indies: these immediate and tangible disasters had shocked the newspapers and back-bench MPs of all parties into demanding that Churchill reform his Government, cutting out the dead – particularly the Tory dead – wood, and stop trying to do too much himself. At this stage there was little demand that Beaverbrook should go; his reputation with the public at any rate stood high. But there was being voiced one insistent demand which made it almost certain that he *would* go. 'Bring back', the cry arose, 'Sir Stafford Cripps from Moscow. Let Cripps, the true representative of the new forces alive in Britain, join the War Cabinet.' Originating from the Left the cry found a ready echo in many Tory circles. Something drastic had to be done.

I cannot recall whether in their correspondence Cripps and Beaverbrook ever started with the pseudo-affectionate 'My dear Max' and 'My dear Stafford'. If so, it was the acme of hypocrisy on both sides. No two men could have been less alike, more calculated to dislike each other — Cripps, the 'sea-green incorruptible', the non-smoker, non-drinker, the exponent of doctrinaire Socialism; Beaverbrook, the lover of good company, the dispenser, in his rare leisure moments, of uncouth cocktails to his galaxy of women, the unbridled champion of capitalism. One always felt that Cripps aspired to be a saint. Beaverbrook revelled in being a sinner. Surely, it would be impossible even for Churchill to get these two natural enemies to run in harness.

So it proved. But Churchill made one attempt. Reluctantly admitting Cripps to his Government he offered his old friend the magniloquent-sounding post of Minister of Production.

It was Thomson who through one long day, and an interminable walk through the yew-tree forest that bordered on Cherkley, argued, pleaded, persuaded, appealed to his master's sense of patriotism, and finally induced him to accept the post. It was duly announced and on the whole was well received. Only a year ago Beaverbrook, the miracle-worker at MAP, had been a name to conjure with. It still had the power to excite the imagination.

So once again the caravan moved on. This time our rooms were a suite in the offices of the War Cabinet. Presiding over this building was a remote cousin of mine, Sir Edward Bridges, who was head of the War Cabinet Secretariat. He was, behind the scene, one of the most powerful men in the country. Thomson, always a stickler for keeping our ends up in the Civil Service world to which we did not really belong, said to me sternly: 'Now, Farrer, no nonsense about our calling Bridges "Sir". We call him "Bridges".' But on this occasion I had the last word. 'Personally,' I replied sweetly, 'I shall call him Cousin Edward.'

The new appointment lasted precisely twelve days. It never really stood a chance. Beaverbrook was supposed to be production overlord. To him overlording spelled dictatorship. It was always 'I want', never 'I ask'. But now there were at least two members of the Cabinet prepared to answer in uncompromising terms 'You shan't'. Cripps and Ernest Bevin were joined in a somewhat unholy alliance, for they had very different views on what the Labour Movement meant. But for the moment dislike of Beaverbrook and all his works united them. To Bevin he was an old opponent, and Cripps had perhaps remembered that Beaverbrook while in Moscow had paid little attention to the British Ambassador. In such a situation Beaverbrook could not operate. For a week he fumed and fretted. The atmosphere in the private office grew sulphurous, and for me fraught with anxiety. Then the fifteenth letter of resignation, despite Thomson's best efforts, sped on its way. This time, rather tartly, it was accepted.

It was the end of a chapter. Though he was later to rejoin the Government, Beaverbrook was never again a member of the War Cabinet, or such a force in Britain's affairs.

7

THE MEANINGLESS MISSION

DURING THE last days in the suite in the Cabinet offices I had added my small voice to Thomson's deeper tones in an effort to persuade Beaverbrook to stay on. I can recall uttering such platitudes as 'The country needs you, Sir,' or, slightly more subtly, 'Mr Churchill will see that you get the power.' To be fair to myself I really did feel that the advantages of Beaverbrook in the Government far outweighed the disadvantages. But I had another, and purely selfish, reason for wanting him to stay.

For nearly two years now I had lived a life of immense excitement and, at one remove, of high drama. I had rubbed shoulders with the great and played at least a tiny part in world-shaking events. Beaverbrook had exalted me far above my previous station in life. Now all this was put in gravest jeopardy. If Beaverbrook left the Government, what was to become of me? The alternatives seemed to be the Army or Fleet Street.

As one of Beaverbrook's secretaries and so technically a civil servant, I had been hitherto classified as in a 'reserved occupation'. Now this shelter from the harsher facts of war was removed from me. Now I was to be subject to the call-up, and very soon I had to present myself at a dingy building somewhere in Islington for an educational test and a medical examination. My answers to the memory and intelligence tests that were set before me must have qualified me for the very lowest grade of private soldier. Never, since I made a complete mess of conducting my one and only case before a High Court judge (he was the brother of Somerset Maugham), had I felt myself so stupid. No matter. On to the Medical Officer. Behind my right ear there lurked a menacing-looking scar, witness to a mastoid operation ten years previously. I had nearly died from the operation. The scar was to preserve me from possible death by shrapnel or bullet. The Medical Officer took one look at it, and pronounced me unfit for military service. Mine not to reason why. Mine not to assure him that the operation had caused no permanent damage, that my hearing was equally good in both ears. I was not a military type.

So it looked like Fleet Street, unless it was to be the sack. Dismissal, however, I did not now fear. My Master had given me indications of a certain growing affection for his unlikely choice of two years ago. Journalism was not so alarming a prospect as the Army, but it would present a daunting challenge which I was ill-equipped to meet. I was scarcely trained at all; only six weeks had intervened between my joining Beaverbrook and his entering the Government. Fleet Street would be for me an uncharted sea full already of first-rate swimmers.

I awaited with anxiety my immediate fate. It took the totally unexpected form of my first visit to the United States.

Though he had left – his critics were saying 'had flounced out of' – the Government, Beaverbrook remained on the closest terms with the Prime Minister. The latter however was anxious to find work for idle hands; he did not, I am convinced, underestimate his friend's capacity for making mischief. He may or may not have heard of an evening, shortly after Beaverbrook's resignation, at Cherkley when the only guest was Sir Arthur Salter, who had recently retired from the Government, but was still an influential backbench Member of Parliament. Sir Arthur was somewhat surprised by the invitation; he was by no means on intimate terms with the ex-Minister of Production. After two cocktails Beaverbrook came to the point. Would Sir Arthur join him in forming an anti-Churchill party? Sir Arthur's answer was brief and to the point. 'No.' The rest of the evening was passed in considerable embarrassment.*

The question has often been asked, did Beaverbrook ever seriously aspire to be Prime Minister in Churchill's place? The only positive evidence I have ever heard in favour of this theory

* This story was told to the author by Sir Arthur, now Lord Salter during a private conversation.

is the approach to Sir Arthur Salter. From my own observation at very close quarters I am convinced that he never did more than flirt with the idea. Some of his cronies in high places – the General Manager of the *Daily Express* among them – encouraged him to go further. Paragraphs did appear in the Press suggesting that he was the man for the job, but when he heard of them he put a stop to them. In his mind he knew that the top job was not on the cards. He had no real political backing. Anthony Eden was Churchill's heir designate. Attlee, the most consistently underrated man in politics, might have carried the country: so might Bevin, but for his complete loyalty before and after the war to the titular head of the Labour Party. Sir Stafford Cripps was, after his return from Russia, seen briefly in some quarters as the nation's saviour, but only briefly. One thing however was certain. None of these powerful figures would have agreed to serve under Beaverbrook, and Beaverbrook knew it. He might blast off to me about 'that damn fellow Churchill', he might throw a fit of sulks when asked to dine at No. 10, he might declaim that he had been right and Churchill wrong over the Malayan disaster, but he always knew that Churchill was the greater man, however much he disliked the knowledge.

Beaverbrook was always faithful, in his fashion, to the man he admired above all others, but in those early days of 1942, with his friend under increasing attack from many quarters, it was a rather peculiar fashion. It was advisable, from Churchill's point of view, to get him out of the country for a while, so he invented an unofficial mission to Washington.

'Invented' is the only word. It was the most meaningless mission of the whole war. Its terms of reference were imprecise in the extreme. Vaguely Beaverbrook was to discuss the question of oil supplies with President Roosevelt and his advisers; that was about all. Why did Beaverbrook accept it? He was in those days in no state to make a clear judgment about anything. His physical reserves were low, his asthma, however self-induced, was proving a real torture. Churchill made it clear that he should undertake a mission and take a holiday as well. The sunshine of Miami Beach or Nassau in the Bahamas beckoned, as the South of France had beckoned two long years ago. Perhaps – he never admitted it to me – he welcomed the chance of private talks with the President, for they were old friends, bound together, amongst other ties, by a shared passion for the works and character of Rudyard Kipling.* He accepted Churchill's invitation.

Then there was a hitch. In answer to a question in the House of Commons, Attlee, the Deputy Prime Minister, made some unintentionally slighting reference to Beaverbrook's forthcoming journey. Beaverbrook blew up; he had been insulted, the mission was off. It was all that damned fellow Churchill. To me this was a bitter blow, for he had told me that I was to accompany him. The thought of a visit to America was excitement enough. Additionally, I was to be given the chance to spread my own little wings. I was to go alone, unprotected by the shield of Thomson. Who knew what prodigies I might perform? Now these hopes were to be dashed. I pleaded with him in vain. He was in his most intractable mood.

There entered at that moment on the scene the Minister of Information. Brendan Bracken was a very tall, ungainly man, with unappetizing sandy hair, and a swiftly growing reputation as a man who knew in wartime what could and could not be published and was persuading British and American correspondents and newspaper proprietors to his point of view. He enjoyed the confidence both of Churchill and Beaverbrook, and now, not for the first time, he acted as successful intermediary. The scene was the Savoy Hotel, where Beaverbrook had established temporary London headquarters. His room faced the Thames; Thomson's and mine faced a dark and dingy well. Nockels was in the temporary position of coming in as a daily help. One morning I encountered the Minister of Information in the passage, watched him enter my master's room. Presently there came therefrom loud cries of argument and protestation. Suddenly the door was thrown open and the two men stood in

* It is strange that Roosevelt, who did so much to undermine the British Empire, should have been so devoted to the works of that Empire's most eloquent propagandist.

the passage. 'I won't, I won't, I won't,' Beaverbrook cried, so
that it seemed the whole Savoy must hear.

'Now Max, now Max.'

'I won't. God damn it, I've been insulted, why should I?'

'Max, do please be reasonable.'

By this time both Thomson and I were awestruck witnesses
to the scene. Then Beaverbrook noticed his audience. The scene
died on us. Brendan Bracken departed, and so, a few days
later, did Beaverbrook and I.

The party was completed by Nockels, and by Senator Elliot.
The Senator had come from New Zealand to assist Beaverbrook
at MAP, where he had never had any clearly defined duties. He
was an old war-horse of the Empire Free Trade days. Of all the
Beaverbrook devotees he was the most unqualified. Like a St
Bernard dog he followed his master around, a barrel of adulation round his neck from which Beaverbrook could drink at
need. He was very kind and rather stupid. He bumbled. Beaverbrook put him in charge of the mission's travel arrangements.
We assembled, the Senator, Nockels and I, one morning early
early in March, at Waterloo, to board a train that was to take
us to Poole Harbour in Dorset, where we were to be joined by
Beaverbrook and to take to the air in a Boeing flying-boat. Some
friends were there to see us off, including Thomson and an old
friend of mine, Armorel Dunne* who had been chief chauffeuse
for Admiral Evans in the MAP days. Nockels was very gracious,
in complete command of the situation. 'How delightful that
you could be here, Mrs Dunne.' As the train pulled out he was
waving regally at the compartment window.

Poole Harbour brought the first shock. The Senator had told
me that the major part of the flying-boat would be reserved for
our use, but as we went on board, it became obvious that every
seat was taken. The plane was crammed with a motley assortment of soldiers, sailors, women with babies, minor diplomats.
Nockels turned pale with alarm. However, I consoled myself

* Her husband, Sir Laurence Dunne, was later to become famous as
Chief Metropolitan Magistrate of London.

with the fact that the first leg of our journey was a very short
one, to Foynes on Ireland's west coast. Perhaps all these
passengers would get off there. The same thought may have
been in Beaverbrook's mind, at least he made no particular fuss.
They did, however, no such thing. When we re-embarked the
plane was as full as ever. A curtain had been rigged up around
the front seat where Beaverbrook was installed; that was all.
Soon from behind the curtain came ominous rumblings.
Nockels emerged to summon the Senator. Presently he too
emerged, visibly shaken, but there was nothing to be done. In
my seat at the back of the plane, as far as possible from my
master, I settled down to try to sleep.

Very early in the morning I was summoned behind the
curtain. What arrangements had been made for our day-stop in
Lisbon? It turned out that the Senator had made none. What
did *I* suggest? (It was becoming apparent that the Senator was
on the way out and I looked dangerously like being on the way
in.) 'Well, Sir,' I replied guilefully, 'I think you will be expected
to stay at the Embassy.'

'Damn it, why should I spend the day with some God damn
Ambassador?'

'It might not be very safe for you to go anywhere else.'

That struck home and, I think, flattered his vanity. I was
gambling on the Embassy sending someone to meet him and on
that someone not including the entourage in the invitation. The
prospect of a free day in Lisbon was very alluring. The gamble
paid off. Beaverbrook went along meekly enough, Nockels, the
Senator and I took a taxi to the Aviz, then the most exclusive
hotel in Lisbon, where we sampled the delights of huge bath-
rooms with mosaic floors, fresh bacon and eggs and above all
oranges, a fruit long unseen and almost forgotten in England.

That evening – we were flying by night to avoid the risk of
German air attack – the other passengers had disappeared. We
were left to fly in luxury to Bathurst, the capital of what was
then Gambia. Here there was another hitch; the Governor had
not been informed that we were arriving. This was probably
not the Senator's fault. There was a sort of semi-secrecy about
our journey, appropriate perhaps to the semi-mission that we

were. But the Senator got the blame. After a delay, during which Beaverbrook fumed and fretted, we were escorted to Government House. After lunch His Excellency sent us off to bathe. From a silver-sandy beach we plunged into what, unknown to us, was a shark-infested sea. Next morning we alighted in the mouth of the river Amazon where we climbed aboard a houseboat (I was by now unofficially in charge of arrangements) where we had breakfast one degree South of the Equator in a humid heat that was almost unbearable. Thence we flew on, unthreatened now by German aircraft, by daylight to Trinidad. Here I managed to repeat the Lisbon tactics; Beaverbrook trotted off meekly enough to Government House while the rest of us enjoyed a free evening in the Queen's Hotel.

The next day's flying took us to the coast of Florida, and for a while it seemed that Miami was for me and Nockels to be our journey's end. It had taken over four days to get there; on her peacetime run the Queen Mary would have been within hailing distance of New York. We repaired to an hotel and there Beaverbrook announced we would stay – though not in a grand hotel but in a modest pension – while he flew on alone to Washington for conversations with the President. We were to await his return. I protested hotly. My nerves on edge after the journey, possessed perhaps by a kind of *folie de grandeur*, I decided that my whole relationship with His Lordship was at stake. Either I was his personal secretary, in which case I ought to be at hand when he was having important talks with the President of the United States, or I was just a piece of luggage to be left in the cloakroom.* Nockels added his protests to mine. Whatever would His Lordship do without his trusted valet? Surprisingly Beaverbrook yielded. Perhaps he disliked the thought of spending the next weeks in the company of two sulky subordinates to whom he was willy-nilly committed. We re-embarked for Baltimore en route for Washington, DC. The Senator came too; at Washington he left us, to make his way back to England.

* I had another reason. In Washington there was working a very old friend whom I had not seen since the war. It would be a golden opportunity to meet him.

In Washington during our two days' stay birth was given to an idea that was to be Beaverbrook's *leitmotif* during all the eighteen months he remained outside the Government. He received while he was there an invitation from the Newspaper Proprietors Association of America to be the principal speaker at their annual banquet; and he discussed, among other things, with Roosevelt and Hopkins what his speech should be about. The result, a month later, was his demand for 'the Second Front'.

This decision taken – I was unaware of it at the time – Beaverbrook flew back to Miami Beach, leaving Nockels and myself to follow by train. It was his revenge for our having made him take us to Washington at all. His intention, he made all too clear later when he was presented by Nockels – in cowardly fashion I delegated this task to him – with the bill, was that we should travel 'coach', sitting up all the way. Our intentions were otherwise. We booked a bedroom each and travelled on the Atlantic Coast Express in great comfort during the thirty-six hour journey through Virginia, the Carolinas, Georgia and Florida. It was a most enjoyable experience, at the end of which we presented ourselves at the luxurious apartment hotel on Miami Beach at which Beaverbrook was staying.

Even without knowledge of those costly bedrooms on the Atlantic Coast Express, he was in his blackest mood. He berated us violently for the slowness of the train, then demanded furiously to know why we thought *we* should be staying in *his* hotel. Why hadn't we got ourselves cheap rooms somewhere in the town? Didn't we realize his was an *unofficial* mission, that he would have to account to the Treasury for every penny spent? Who did we think we were? We listened in silence, our mien, as I am sure Nockels would agree, that of penitent schoolboys. All we could do was hope to ride out the storm, as Nockels in particular had ridden out many another. Suddenly it passed. 'Ah, God, I suppose you'd better have your way. Get yourselves rooms here. And Farrer, take a letter to Brendan Bracken. Nockels, you've lost two of my white silk shirts.' The sun was shining again.

The sun was shining on Miami Beach too, and this is the only explanation I can give for his sudden outburst. Here he was in his beloved sunshine, *and here he ought not to be*. What were the people back home saying? That he was an *embusqué*, that he had deserted the ship. He ought never to have come. It was all the fault of that damned fellow Churchill. I am only guessing, but I think I am guessing right. Often in the days that followed the same theme recurred in his conversations with me – What am I doing here?

At the hotel on Miami Beach Beaverbrook had several visitors. They included John Winant the American Ambassador and Lord Halifax the British Ambassador, and ex-Ambassador Joseph Kennedy, still fairly close to Roosevelt to whose initial Presidential campaign he had contributed so many million dollars. I was not present at their discussions, but since I was by now privy to the projected Second Front speech it was not hard to guess that these visitors were uttering cautionary or, from Kennedy, encouraging words. The speech was beginning to dominate Beaverbrook's thought, and I was kept busy preparing headings, assembling facts and figures. In my spare time I explored Miami. I can remember a vast pool in which giant turtles wallowed, rows and rows of Mexican-style villas, each with its bed of flaming cannas and air of appalling vulgarity. I took a violent and self-righteous dislike to this millionaires' playground where the sun shone but the wind nearly always blew. It seemed to mock the drab austerity of wartime Britain.

After about ten days we moved on to another seaside resort, Sea Island on the coast of Georgia. Here the villas were luxurious but lacked ostentation. One of them had been lent to Beaverbrook together with a negress who cooked Southern food in a way I have never seen equalled. The beach was deserted, for it was out of season. Behind it were sandhills and behind them stretched mile upon mile of decaying cotton plantations – a luxuriant green – and tumble-down farmsteads. It was a strangely beautiful landscape, reminding one that for all her riches America had her Achilles heel of poverty. Here too, for at least three-quarters of the day, it was the speech, the whole speech, and nothing but the speech.

Beaverbrook set enormous store by it. For this there were two reasons, the one more creditable than the other. Every task this phenomenon of a man undertook he pursued with an almost evangelic enthusiasm. It had been thus with Empire Free Trade; it had been thus at MAP; it was to be thus with the agitation for the Second Front. Each was launched when he was in the political wilderness; and this underlines one of his weaknesses. In his search for the limelight he was too often heedless of the feasibility of what he was advocating. He knew in March 1942 all the secrets of the British Service Ministries; he knew that to attempt a Second Front in Europe that year would be an almost totally unacceptable risk. No matter, here was a cause and he would give the clarion call that would make him its leader.

There was another facet to his highly emotional approach to this subject. The Second Front was what Stalin was demanding. He had become in Moscow Stalin's friend. Now he would become the great Russian leader's advocate before the British and American people and thereby regain a position of real power and influence in the affairs of the Allies. Such, I believe, was the complex emotion and reasoning that led him to start a campaign which led to serious strains in Anglo-American relations, which caused first elation, then disappointment, finally rage to the men in the Kremlin, which created a violent division in British public opinion, and the end result of which was precisely nil.

For the time being, however, and indeed, as it turned out, for many months, it gave him something to do. Day after day he worked on the speech, in the villa, on the beach, discussing it with me on walks along the shore. It obsessed him. I would make occasional critical comments, suggest a more polished phrase, query a figure he wanted to quote. I wrote to Thomson, asking for confirmation of some facts which Beaverbrook wanted to use, and for additional material. It struck me as I did so that, so closely had we worked together, this was the first occasion we had had to write to each other. His answer came back, and its opening sentence marked, I feel, the final cementing of our friendship and alliance. It began 'My dear David'. Those were the days when Christian names, though bandied about freely enough among Cabinet Ministers, meant to ordinary people friendship or the desire to achieve it. Today five minutes' conversation at a cocktail party and I find I am 'David' or, if I am talking to an American, all too often 'Dave'. It was not thus in 1942. For two years, working in daily contact, we had called each other 'Thomson' and 'Farrer'. Now 'David' from Thomson really meant something, and 'George' was used by 'David' by return of post.

Beaverbrook was obsessed by the speech. He was almost as obsessed by what Churchill would think. He had very few illusions. 'He won't like it, will he?'

'No, Sir, I don't think he will.'

'You think I oughtn't to make it, is that it?'

'Oh, no, Sir. I think you *ought* to make it" – sycophant Farrer hard at work.

'The President will like it, though.'

'Yes, Sir, I'm sure he will.'

'Alright. Now give me those figures.'

He was, indeed, very like a naughty schoolboy preparing for an escapade which he knows will earn him a caning from the Head. At times I am sure he confessed to himself that he was up to mischief, and he was certainly nervous of his reception, if he delivered the speech, when he got home. But the mischief proved irresistible, and, he could reassure himself, the President himself had as good as put him up to it. He intended to show it to him before delivering it.

Before this, however, there had occurred a splendidly farcical interlude. It had been originally planned that we should leave Sea Island by car for Jacksonville where we would take a plane for Washington. Almost at the last moment Beaverbrook decided that he wanted to go by train. I telephoned the station at Jacksonville for reservations, only to be told that the night train to Washington was fully booked. 'I am speaking,' I said, 'on behalf of Lord Beaverbrook.' 'Hold on a minute,' replied the other end, and then 'It can be arranged.' All unsuspecting I reported success. We were to join the train at the wayside station some thirty miles away that served Sea Island. In due course we arrived there as dusk was falling and were cere-moniously conducted to the rear end of the platform.

Now Beaverbrook – though it did not prevent him from staying at the most expensive hotel on Miami Beach and later in the Towers apartments of the Waldorf Astoria – was acutely sensitive about the financial aspects of his journey. He was terrified of being accused, in the American or British Press, of overspending public moneys on a purely 'unofficial' mission. Hence his attempt to drive us into cheap lodgings in Miami, and his displeasure when Nockels finally presented him with the bill for our luxury railway journey. Presently the train was signalled and as it drew into the platform I could see that every compartment was bulging with passengers. The rear coach stopped opposite us, the conductor greeted us with an obeisance, and I jumped in ahead of Beaverbrook. As I went along the corridor a horrible suspicion entered my mind. Hastily I almost shoved the following Beaverbrook into his combined bedroom and sitting room compartment, pushed a by now bewildered Nockels in after him and shut the door. Then I investigated further. My suspicion was all too well-founded. We were the only people in the coach. It had been attached to the train for Beaverbrook's special benefit; for all I knew the train had made a special stop to pick him up.

Presently Nockels emerged, having put his master to bed. I explained to him the ghastly predicament. Nockels assured me that the now couchant ex-Minister had as yet no suspicions. But what of the morning? Nockels rose splendidly to the occasion. 'My dear boy, it's simple' – he paused for effect.

'How do you mean simple,' – I was badly rattled – 'he's bound to find out in the morning.'

'Dear boy, when are we due in Washington?'

'About eight-thirty.'

'Then about a quarter past eight you and I start stamping about the corridor, talking loudly, banging our suitcases, up and down.'

'But when we actually arrive?'

Nockels had thought that one out too. 'I'll tell his probably sleepy Lordship that it'll be much better to wait till the other passengers have gone. You must make the noises of their going.'

It might work, but I spent a largely sleepless night, wondering what would be my fate if it didn't. It did, though the coach's conductor clearly thought that Lord Beaverbrook was accompanied by two lunatics. He got a generous tip. Beaverbrook descended to the platform at Washington unaware of the enormity that had been perpetrated in his name. We proceeded, the three of us, in amity to the Mayflower Hotel.

In Washington Beaverbrook showed the draft of his speech to President Roosevelt. He told me that he had cleared it with him almost line by line. I have not the slightest reason to doubt his word. At that time General George Marshall, head of the American Chiefs of Staff, and Harry Hopkins were in London, urging on Churchill the need for some operations in Western Europe before the year's end, and being stoutly resisted by Churchill and his Chiefs of Staff. (The Americans at this stage were almost totally unversed in the problems of logistics and apparently unaware that all Britain's best fighting troops were committed in the Western Desert.) What could better suit the President's book at this stage than a trumpet call from a powerful ex-Cabinet Minister in his support? We proceeded, Beaverbrook in nervously truculent mood, to New York.

My first view of a city that has ever since fascinated me was from the air, as dusk was falling. It was electrifying, the skyscrapers, the whole city, were ablaze with lights. To a traveller accustomed since 1 September 1939 to the Stygian gloom of blackout London, the sight seemed incredible. The war seemed a million miles away.

In his suite on the thirty-ninth floor of the Waldorf Towers Beaverbrook put the final touches to the speech. In its penultimate version it contained a peroration provided by me of which I was rather proud, and on which Beaverbrook had complimented me. It ended:

> Nor shall the Sword sleep in his hand
> Till he has built Jerusalem
> In *Europe's* green and pleasant land.

The reference was of course to our great leader Churchill, a sop to Cerberus. But on the morning of the speech Beaverbrook struck it out. I protested. 'It's no good, Farrer. They'll give me a great deal to drink, and I shall end up "Nor shall the Shord shleep in my hand".'

The speech, even without my peroration, made headlines all over America and Britain. It has been often reprinted in full, more often resumé'd. It is unnecessary now to do more than point out that it contained one giant paradox. Part of it was devoted to extravagant praise of Churchill, but the major part, the part that caught the imagination, was devoted to an impassioned plea for a policy to which Churchill was totally opposed. ('Strike now, for Britain and for our gallant Russian allies. Strike now for victory. Let us open a Second Front in 1942.') It was, however, to the immediate audience to which it was addressed, a resounding success. Beaverbrook could make very bad speeches, and very good speeches; it depended almost entirely on his audience. That evening in the ballroom of the Waldorf Astoria, the audience was entirely to his liking. It was comprised of men who had followed his own profession, newspaper owners, to give only one example, like Henry Luce, whose magazines had in peacetime world-wide circulation. But none of them had risen to the political heights from which this Canadian-born British citizen spoke to them. They provided a setting of admiration, tinged perhaps with envy. To Beaverbrook it was meat and drink.

The next morning, after a cursory look at the newspapers, I congratulated him warmly. 'You were magnificent, Sir.'

'Ah, God, Farrer, it was lucky I didn't have to say "Nor shall the Sword". How did it go?'

'It was magnificent.'

'I wonder what that fellow Churchill will say.'

In point of fact, I had never heard the speech at all. Having escorted him safely to the reception committee at the doorway of the ballroom, I had slipped away to join two friends. It was too good an opportunity to miss. We spent a delightful, carefree evening, while I should have had my ears glued to the wireless on the thirty-ninth floor. But after all, I knew the speech by heart.

Nor did Nockels hear it. He was too busy ministering to the alcoholic needs of a group of Beaverbrook cronies, who had not been invited to the banquet and had assembled in our master's suite. Towards one in the morning Nockels wearied of his task and left the cronies to their own devices. When Beaverbrook returned there was a blazing row. 'God damn it, why can't you look after my guests, who in hell do you think you are?' and much more in that strain. Nockels really had no answer. But an hour later Beaverbrook called for him. The two men faced each other in their pyjamas. Beaverbrook handed Nockels a note. 'This is from me to you.' It read as follows:

DEAR NOCKELS,

I could not possibly manage without your help. You do not need to make any explanation about bad temper, *I have more than you*.

The simple fact is that I have a great affection for you and will never think you rude or rough.

Yours ever,
Beaverbrook.

That morning the telephones were ringing, the telegrams arriving. From the President, by telephone, approval. From American and Canadian friends, and from the General Manager of the *Daily Express*, warm congratulations. But from a certain 'Former Naval Person'* a request that was almost a command that Beaverbrook should return forthwith to London. In any case the deed had been done, the campaign for a Second Front launched in spectacular fashion. There was nothing to keep him in America, back home fresh opportunities might await him. It was in Britain that his new venture must be pursued. We packed our bags.

This time, however, there was no question of going half way round the world to reach England. We flew to Bermuda, thence we were scheduled to fly direct to Lisbon. Only one longer flight had ever been attempted, when three months before

---

* I have never understood why Churchill adopted this transparently thin disguise in his trans-Atlantic messages to the President and others. No German could for an instant be in doubt who the 'former naval person' was.

Churchill, with Beaverbrook and the Chiefs of Staff, had flown 3,300 miles from Bermuda to Plymouth; Bermuda to Lisbon was two hundred miles less. There was something immensely reassuring about those (by modern standards) elephantine flying boats, and as we took off in a great whirl of spray, I felt no qualms about the journey ahead. Half an hour later I noticed a stream of vapour coming from one of the starboard engines. It increased steadily in volume. Then it seemed to me that we were turning in our tracks. Soon Bermuda came again into view. As we circled round and round the island word was passed along that one engine had failed and that we must jettison a thousand gallons of petrol before it would be safe to land. We landed safely and repaired to the hotel I thought I had left for ever. Beaverbrook bore the delay with remarkable equanimity. For myself I could not help wondering what would have happened had the engine failed not half an hour but ten hours after take-off. There was all too little need to wonder.

Thirty-six hours later we were off again, a replacement engine having arrived, I think from Baltimore. In the middle of the night I awoke to realize that we must be somewhere over the mid-Atlantic, at least a thousand miles from land. Resolutely I put the thought away and went to sleep again. Dawn was just breaking when we landed in the mouth of the Tagus. As we left the flying-boat I asked the Captain how much fuel we had left on landing. 'Exactly half-an-hour's flying time' was the reply. I am afraid the answer gave me an entirely spurious feeling of having taken part in a unique, nay heroic, adventure. That evening we flew on to England. This time the plane was empty, the landing in Poole Harbour uneventful. The Southern Railway's slow (it was called semi-fast) train to Waterloo was a sad comedown after the delights and excitements of the Atlantic Coast Express.

8

I COULD WRITE A BOOK

DURING BEAVERBROOK'S absence in America Churchill's position apparently, and his standing in the country certainly, had declined. It seemed at times that he was the only man in Britain who remained convinced that he was still master of his fate. Disaster was striking everywhere. The whole of the Far East had been lost, including Burma; the Indian Congress was refusing to help defend the vast sub-continent which it aspired to rule; the Australians were virulent in their criticism of the loss of Singapore. In Libya there was at best stalemate, and on the high seas the toll on British merchant shipping mounted daily. Nearer home the German battle cruisers Scharnhorst and Gneisenau had sailed from Brest with impunity the length of the English Channel back to safety in a German harbour. Public morale was at its lowest since the beginning of the war. It seemed that we were losing it faster *with* the Americans than without them.

Faced by this mood of gloom and uncertainty, criticized in Parliament by both the Left and the Right, Churchill had now to welcome back to the country his former colleague, bearing aloft a banner with a strange device. 'Welcome' is hardly the right word: to Churchill the banner was totally unacceptable. Only a few days previously he had refused the suggestion of General Marshall and Hopkins that he should unfurl it himself.

The relations of Churchill and Beaverbrook were frostier during the next two months than at any other period of the war. Brendan Bracken worked hard as an intermediary, but it was uphill work. Never far from Churchill's thoughts was the desire to re-employ Beaverbrook in some sort of official position. The Washington Embassy had been mentioned, but there

Lord Halifax was being an unexpected success. The fox-hunting, high Anglican aristocrat was most things the Americans might be expected to dislike; instead they respected his refusal to be anything but himself. The Moscow Embassy ? But now Moscow was ruled out as well. It was impossible to consider an Ambassador who would propound a military strategy to which his Prime Minister was opposed, and to imagine that Beaverbrook would stay silent was to imagine a miracle. For the time being he must remain outside the inner circle of Churchill's advisers; the visits to No. 10 grew few and far between.

With this state of affairs Beaverbrook professed himself content. It left him free to pursue his own campaign and, since he was out of office, to use his newspapers to further its progress. Leading articles began to appear in the *Daily* and *Sunday Express* and the *Evening Standard*, proclaiming in that semi-biblical language the leader writers were apt to employ when promoting one of their owner's causes, the benefits that would multiply from a landing on the coast of France, the shame of standing idly by while our great ally bled almost to death. I myself wrote an article in that same sense for the *Daily Express*. I re-read it today with a certain sense of shame. The same newspaper organized a rally at the London Hippodrome; later Beaverbrook spoke to a mass open-air audience outside the City Hall in Birmingham. It was all heady stuff and for the time being it gained him a large number of followers. They were not however followers who would be likely to have much influence on Government circles. Beaverbrook, the self-made millionaire, the fervent Imperialist, found himself for a brief period that spring almost in the position of the leader of the Far Left. The Communists, the crypto-Communists, the idealists on the left of the orthodox Labour Party, these were the elements in the country to whom the Second Front campaign appealed, as it did to some extent to the workers at the factory bench. 'Make tanks for Russia' Beaverbrook cried, oblivious, it seemed, that British troops had urgent need of them in the Western Desert, and production did increase.

It was a strange spectacle. At times I wondered whether I should yet see my employer on the public platform, swathed in a red flag. There was no doubt about his sincerity. The campaign was, of course, his only immediate way of remaining in the national limelight, but to maintain that this was his only motive would be to do him a grave injustice. He had hypnotized himself into believing that what he was advocating was the surest and swiftest way to victory. To his advocacy he brought all the remarkable force of his driving energy, and for a while his campaign seemed to prosper.

Then came the news of the fall of Tobruk (it was given to him as he mounted the platform for his Birmingham speech). It was for the man in the street the most humiliating incident in the whole war – worse than the fall of Singapore, worse than the escape of the German cruisers. It caused Churchill to wobble temporarily on his throne. It put an effective end to the campaign for the Second Front. The campaign rumbled and grumbled on through the rest of 1942, and there were signs of a revival when Beaverbrook realised that there would be no landings in France even in 1943. But the public mood had changed; after Tobruk there were other, more immediate things to attend to.

Churchill was in Washington when Tobruk fell. He returned at once to face the most hostile House of Commons of the whole war. Right wing and Left wing were after his blood, only the centre (comprised largely of Ministers, junior Ministers and Parliamentary Private Secretaries) held firm. A vote of censure was tabled. At one period in World War 1 Marshal Foch, the Frenchman who was in supreme command of the Allies in the West, declared: 'My right is retreating, my left is in disarray, *I am attacking.*' Churchill now adopted the same tactics. He refused a belated offer to withdraw the vote of censure. He would counter-attack, and to assist him he would ask the aid of his old friend. Would Beaverbrook make the chief speech in the House of Lords, and would he defend the Government's record and attack its critics? There was not a moment's delay in saying yes. Gone at once were the memories of recent bickerings and recrimination, their departure hastened, I think, by a certain sense of guilt. The man he admired most in the world was in trouble, and that was all that mattered.* There were to be further quarrels and disagreements ahead, but never again did the clouds threaten to obscure the sun, as they had in those few months of 1942.

The friendship was restored, but there was no immediate prospect of the junior partner rejoining his senior's Government. Beaverbrook maintained vigorously, even violently, whenever I told him he ought to go back, that he did not want to. Perhaps – – . But the factors that had caused him to leave it anyway still prevailed. The power of Cripps had not yet begun to wane, the power of Bevin would never wane. There was no executive post which Churchill could give him. So, with the future obscure, with little prospect of active participation in the war's conduct, he decided, for a while at least, to live in the past.

One morning at Cherkley Beaverbrook said to me: 'How would you like to write a book?'

I was by now long accustomed to his unpredictability. I showed little surprise as I replied: 'Very much, Sir. What about?'

'The Ministry of Aircraft Production, of course.'

Two things became immediately clear to me. 'How would you like to' meant 'I intend that you should', and for 'Ministry' read 'the first Minister'. I made suitable noises about my unfitness for the task, which were brushed aside. We were both already aware that, though the pen that wrote might be mine, the inspiration would be largely Beaverbrook's. So began for me a task that was to take me nine months, and was to provide me with the nearest approximation to a fixed daily routine that I was to know in all the years I worked for him.

Though Stornoway House had been replaced by a top floor flat at Brook House in Park Lane, which was in turn to give way to a more luxurious penthouse in Arlington House, next door to the Ritz Hotel, Beaverbrook at this period lived almost entirely at Cherkley. It was to this Edwardian-style mansion on the outskirts of Leatherhead that every morning I would repair. A commuter in reverse, I would catch a train at Waterloo and

* For a full account of this episode, see G. M. Thomson, *Vote of Censure*, 1968, pp. 190 *et seq.*

endure the slow torture of a journey of eighteen miles which the Southern Railway managed to achieve in fifty-eight minutes. All trains to Leatherhead were stopping trains. They stopped ten times, and the stops must in duration have almost equalled the 'go's'. Concentrating on the daily newspapers, whose leading articles I must digest for my master, I tried not to look at the dreary outcrop of suburbia through which we passed. Yet names like Earlsfield and Worcester Park are graven on my mind. At last it was Leatherhead ('change for the Effingham line') and his Lordship's chauffeur waiting. Five minutes later I was at the doors of Cherkley.

Here I would invariably be met by Nockels, and would ask anxiously:

'What's the form?'

'We are in a fairly reasonable mood,' or alternatively 'Stinking, dear boy, stinking.'

It was Nockels's custom to greet any visitor to Cherkley at the front door, no matter whether he was a junior personal secretary or a Cabinet Minister. 'How are you?' – 'Sir', if it were one of the high-ups – 'How nice to see you.' Discovering him in the act one day, Beaverbrook grew furious, bade Nockels abandon this habit. 'God damn it, you act as if you owned the place.' Nockels desisted. Shortly afterwards Sir Walter Citrine, at that time the most important of the Trade Union leaders, arrived for dinner. 'Hullo, Nockels, how are you?' said Sir Walter. 'Why didn't you greet me at the door?' Thereafter, by tacit consent, Nockels re-assumed his welcoming role.

After he had welcomed me I would proceed to the secretaries' room and await the summons. Very often, if it were fine, he would be sitting outside his library window, facing the sheltered rose garden. Always there would be a telephone by his side.

'Get me Christiansen,' and then, when the connection had been made: 'Chris, that's a fine paper today. Anything going on?' – a question usually followed by Beaverbrook telling his Editor the latest news. Or the conversation might start: '*Mr* Christiansen, the *Daily Express* is a fine newspaper, but – – ' One could always tell. The prefix Mr boded no good for the Editor on the other end of the line. 'Farrer here tells me the *Daily Mail* carried a story about that German submarine; didn't you think it worth covering?' Often I felt I was unwittingly stabbing poor Christiansen in the back. He was the best editor the *Daily Express* ever had: he was also sorely harassed by his employer.

With Michael Foot, recently appointed Editor of the *Evening Standard*, however, it was always the Christian name, whether it was praise or criticism that followed, and the criticism when it came – and this was rarely – was less that of an employer rebuking an employee than of a father chiding a much loved child. He had for Michael Foot a deeper affection that for anyone who worked for him while I was there. He had lent him a cottage on the Cherkley Estate, and on most evenings, after he returned from London, Foot would dine and talk late into the night with his employer, acting almost as his eyes and ears, regaling him with the latest political gossip. In particular he would keep him abreast of opinion in the Left Wing circles, increasingly dominated by the Welsh oratory of Aneurin Bevan, in which he moved. Later, after the war, when he had become a Member of Parliament, Foot made an impassioned political attack on Beaverbrook and all he stood for. Beaverbrook was deeply hurt. I have never, I think, seen him so upset. 'God damn it,' he said to me, 'I never thought that fellow Foot would do that to me.' But the wound healed, perhaps the glowing tribute Foot paid him at the dinner to celebrate his seventieth birthday effected the final cure. He remained to the end of Beaverbrook's life a 'favourite son'.

The newspapers disposed of, and my views on current events solicited and usually rejected, I would read him the previous day's instalment of the book. It was a strange quirk in him that he found it easier to apply his mind to a subject when he was being read to than when he was reading. If I had stayed the night at Cherkley and he was going to London the next morning, I had to read the morning's leading articles to him while the car swayed along the Kingston by-pass. This task gave my successor such acute car-sickness that he had to resign. The instalment over, Beaverbrook would fire suggestions and facts at me with a machine-gun rapidity that taxed my apology for shorthand to its limits. I would then retire – he usually gave

me notes for letters as well – to the secretaries' room and work
until lunchtime.

Lunch was often eaten *à deux*. In that case it was a frugal
meal – I got extremely tired of chicken in any form or shape –
eaten to the accompaniment of a monologue, in which his
nimble mind skipped from subject to subject while mine panted
breathlessly behind. From time to time I would interpose an
interjection – 'I couldn't agree more, Sir' or more daringly 'I
wonder if that's *quite* true' – then the flow, if he was in a good
mood, would be resumed; but there were bad days when lunch
would proceed in silence. It was neither easy nor wise for me
to start a conversation on my own. He would either ignore it
or tear it to pieces.

Then to work again. Sometimes I would sit with him on the
terrace, discussing the book or some article he wanted me to
write for one of the newspapers. The view was magnificent,
across the valley known as the Dorking Gap (through which, it
had been anticipated, the Germans would channel their main
attack on London) to the wooded slopes of the North Downs
opposite. It was a panorama that belied our nearness to London.
I never saw his Lordship more at peace with himself and the
world than when, his brows knitted against the sunlight, he
contemplated this prospect before him.

More often, however, I would return to my room and resume
my labours. It might be that between four and four-thirty I
would be summoned to accompany him on his afternoon walk.
Usually, however, he left me in peace. This half-hour was anyway a key point in my day. It was an unwritten law that, if I
were not actually with him at the time, I could leave for
London at half-past five. His customary walk took an hour.
Therefore if he set out before four-thirty, my freedom was in
jeopardy. It was a joyous moment when Nockels reported that
the walk had started late. My staunch ally in so many things,
he always made sure that the car was at the door on the stroke
of half-past five. From the window of the secretaries' room one
could see the bend of the drive down which his Lordship would
return. 'Sister Anne,' (Brother Nockels in this case), 'Sister Anne,
can you see anyone coming?'

Another unwritten law was that if I were still with him at seven o'clock, I would stay to dinner and usually for the night. Dinner normally brought a guest: 'one of his women' – the phrase was Nockels's – perhaps a visiting American like Roy Howard of the Scripps-Howard chain of newspapers, often Brendan Bracken and Averell Harriman, Sir Walter Citrine, on occasions Randolph Churchill whom I once saw dominate by sheer rudeness even a table presided over by Beaverbrook – 'stop talking rubbish, Max' (the word he used was more vulgar) – old friends from MAP days like Patrick Hennessy, Lord Bennett from his house across the valley, aging now, but still fatherly and friendly to 'little f', Valentine Castlerosse, in all but bulk a shadow of the man who had invented the gossip column, a character for whom the war had destroyed everything he enjoyed doing, but good company still. Whatever the company the post-prandial entertainment never varied. Around ten o'clock Beaverbrook and his guests adjourned to the private cinema.

Watching a film was one of Beaverbrook's few recreations, and it must be added that if he liked a film he did not mind how many times he watched it. Legend has it that he saw Marlene Dietrich in *Destry Rides Again* fifty-two times; I know that I saw it on six different occasions. 'See what the boys in the back room will have,' he would shout gleefully as he sat among his guests in the raised tier at the back of the cinema, oblivious of the fact that one or two of them, in the luxurious seating accommodation provided, were sleeping off the brandy. As soon as we were seated the staff filed in, led by Major-Domo Nockels. Mabel, head housekeeper, followed, then Chef, then Miss Evans, elderly and prim, retained as honorary housekeeper from the days of the first Lady Beaverbrook; Creasy the butler, a sworn foe of Nockels, William the head footman and supernumaries male and female.

Mabel was a sturdy, uncompromising figure who ran her side of the household with masterly efficiency. I believe that, secretly, Beaverbrook was scared of her. Certainly she had a vocabulary of swear words fully equal to his own. Later she was to marry Nockels and to live happily ever after. It was Beaverbrook's fond belief that in admitting the staff to the cinema, he was giving them a treat. Nockels felt otherwise. They would, he told me, have preferred their beds to Marlene Dietrich.

'One of his women.' Often two or three were present at his dinner table. Since the death of his wife fifteen years earlier, there had been many women in Beaverbrook's life. They satisfied in him the need not just for sex but for uncritical admiration. Most of them gave it in full measure. They found this, by normal standards, ugly man almost irresistible. Where women were concerned he was a whole magnetic field to himself. One evening I was dining with an old friend in a London restaurant. A page-boy brought her a message, which read 'Would Mrs — care to come down to Cherkley. Lord Beaverbrook's car is waiting outside.' She got up and left me at once. To each of these women in his circle he gave a present on *his*, not their, birthday. It was perhaps an interesting sidelight on his very complicated character.

But of all of them only two, at least in my time, exercised any influence over him, and in each case that influence was wholly for the good. Jean Grantley* I knew only as she impinged on Beaverbrook's life. She was beautiful and talented. At the start of the war she had at once given up her easy social life and gone to work full-time at the factory bench. Beaverbrook was devoted to her, and on occasions treated her extremely badly. On one occasion he almost went too far. After a bitter quarrel shortly before the war, in which he was wholly in the wrong, she left Cherkley, determined to break off the liaison. She booked accommodation in the Golden Arrow for Paris. Somehow he heard of this. Pulling all his strings, he got a message to her at Dover just before she boarded the Channel steamer. She relented, and returned to Cherkley. Thereafter she gave him the sort of unselfish devotion of which this often tortured, twisted man was so much in need. The day when he learned of her

* She was Jean Kinloch and married Richard Norton, who subsequently inherited the title of Baron Grantley.

death was the only occasion when I saw him break down utterly and weep.

Of Lily Ernst I find it difficult to write, for she became a dear friend. But no account of the man I knew would be complete without her. She was a Hungarian by birth, and when Beaverbrook first met her she was a dancer in a ballet company in the South of France. In 1936, at the time when Hitler marched into Austria, she was living in Vienna. Realizing the danger that she might well be in – she was soon to hear that both her parents had vanished into the infamous concentration camp at Auschwitz – Beaverbrook arranged, through the *Daily Express* correspondent in Vienna, that she should come at once to London, where she was living at the outbreak of war. During the panic internment of hundreds of innocent aliens that followed the fall of France, he helped to preserve her liberty. Thenceforth she was very frequently at Cherkley, or with him in London. Though she knew, and was fully a match for, most of his political and social friends, she kept herself, with few exceptions, somehow aloof from them; it was to Beaverbrook that she owed her allegiance, and to no one else. She was completely devoted to his interests and because he knew it he could talk with her about everything with no holds barred. People used to say that he gave his full confidence to no one. Lily Ernst was the exception. She was a sort of safety-valve. Besides, he loved her deeply. Lily was (and still is) dark, slim, immensely graceful. Sometimes in those days she had an almost waif-like look that betrayed a character of strong integrity. She spoke, in a lilting accent, a delightful and often very funny form of fractured English. It reminded me of Yvonne Arnaud, and I suspect that like that famous comedienne, she preserved it, for the delight it gave, long after she had mastered the language. At Cherkley she would spend many an hour, making life for me, after a nagging morning or a black-avised lunch, become bearable again. Later she married. The initial shock to him was very great. But once he realized how supremely happy and successful her marriage was proving, resentment and jealously vanished. Till his death they remained the closest of friends. Anyway,

throughout the trials and tribulations of the war years Beaverbrook would have been lost without her.

Throughout that summer and autumn of 1942, with El
Alamein, Stalingrad, the naval battle of Midway Island in the
Pacific, and the Anglo-American landings in North Africa, the
tide of war at last began to turn. But Beaverbrook sat mainly
on the sidelines while he and I got down to the task of writing
about MAP. In one respect *The Sky's The Limit* bore a curious
resemblance to the only other book I had then written. This
was a novel about life in prison and its after-effects. I had never
been nearer prison than a police court fine for using insulting
words and behaviour at the London Palladium. The chief
character was based on a young ex-criminal who had worked
for me after his release from prison. Without him, as the dedica-
tion announced, the novel 'would not and could not have been
written'. The same applied to *The Sky's The Limit*. Without
Beaverbrook's documents, promptings, advice and criticism
there could have been no book. To that extent he was its joint
author, as he always meant to be.

Before I started on the task Beaverbrook told me that he
wanted to be portrayed, like one of his heroes Oliver Cromwell,
'warts and all'. I like to think he thought he meant it, but it is
only a highly dispassionate, self-critical man who is likely to
admit in print that he possesses any warts at all, and Beaverbrook was not such a character. As the writing of the book
proceeded I was reminded more and more of the story of another
famous man who was writing his autobiography. A subordinate
who had read the first draft suggested that it might be a good
thing to give just a few examples of incidents when he had
been in the wrong. 'My dear fellow,' came the reply, 'this is
not a work of fiction.' As he looked back on his year as Minister
of Aircraft Production Beaverbrook quite honestly could not
see a single wart.

So there began a long unfought battle between author and
subject matter. Knowing the extent of his achievements, I hated
the idea of over-egging the Beaverbrook pudding. To give a true,

a convincing picture of the remarkable man he then was, there simply had to be some warts. Perhaps it is true that no man is a hero to his own secretary (or, *pace* Nockels, to his own valet). Beaverbrook was never to me of heroic stature – he was far too human – but he had been supremely the right man in the right place at the right time. From the start I was engaged in a struggle to impose some of my own conception of him upon his own.

But for one factor, unrealized by Beaverbrook, the struggle would have been lost. Alone I was no match for him. Often when he was being particularly overweening or demanding, he drove me to mutter to myself 'I'll show the little bastard', but I very seldom made any attempt to do so. Just occasionally, as on the occasion when he berated me in front of his Council at MAP and I lost my temper, risked the sack and survived, I stood up to him, but he had an uncanny knack of knowing just how far he could go. He sensed too, I think, that in those days I would sacrifice great chunks of my self-respect in order to make sure of remaining in his employ. It was fortunate indeed for me, for the book, and for Beaverbrook's reputation, that George Malcolm Thomson was lurking behind the scenes.

To George, whenever opportunity offered, I would show the latest instalment. He would make suggestions, offer criticisms, suggest amendments all designed to achieve our common purpose – a picture not devoid of warts and for that very reason redounding to our master's greater credit. I would then redraft and present the amended version for Beaverbrook's inspection, pretending, God help me!, that it was the fruit of my own second thoughts. He would always at first demur, and sometimes the original wartless version would be re-instated. More often than not, however, he would show the new version to Thomson. 'Farrer seems to think – – ' George would consider the typescript pages as if he had never seen them before, pause for reflection, and then persuasively, almost diffidently, indicate that *perhaps* Farrer was right. These were Machiavellian tactics, but by and large they worked. I remember in particular an early and very formidable hurdle which George helped me to jump. In the draft of the very first chapter I had, as I have already mentioned, written: 'Churchill persisted in his offer. To his personal secretaries Beaverbrook protested with increasing vehemence that he would not take office, and with each protest the secretaries became more certain that he would.' Beaverbrook did not at first like this passage at all. It showed an all too frivolously cynical attitude on the part of his secretaries. George, with some assistance on this occasion from me, persuaded him to the contrary. It showed not only their affection for their master but their relief that he would take office. Besides, it showed him as a very human human being. Beaverbrook yielded the point.

The least I could do, when the book was finished, was to dedicate it

To GMT
Who will know why

Beaverbrook asked GMT a little querulously why he should know why. GMT replied evasively that he supposed it was because we had worked so closely together in the MAP days. Beaverbrook was always suspicious of collusion between his two personal secretaries. Little did he know how often, during the writing of the book and at other times too, it took place.

The Sky's The Limit was finished early in 1943. During all the time it was being written Beaverbrook was 'in waiting'. Constantly he protested that nothing would induce him to rejoin the Government, he was happier outside it. 'Methinks the lady doth protest too much.' It was incredible to me that so keen a mind, so quick a brain could be kept indefinitely on the sidelines. Beaverbrook was seeing Churchill very often and was, though he never admitted it to me, I am sure privy to most of the Government's plans and actions. It was an anomalous situation. He was disliked by some of the Prime Minister's chief colleagues. Yet, rather than have him half in these men would reluctantly prefer that he should be all in. At one moment Beaverbrook toyed with the idea of going into outright opposition, a sure sign of his feelings of frustration, but as usual the pull of Churchill was too strong. Then on 1 April 1943 he returned from a visit to No. 10 telling Thomson that the Prime Minister had offered him a glass of brandy and a job.

'Did you take the brandy?' 'Yes.' 'And the job?' 'Yes.'

He was to be Leader of the House of Lords; it seemed that our caravan would start rolling again. And then, suddenly, Churchill took him with him on another visit to Washington. Had he just been perpetrating an April Fools' Day joke?

9

A RETURN VISIT

THE EVENTS of the first days of April 1943 remain to me still shrouded in mystery. First, Beaverbrook was to rejoin the Government, and I rejoiced. Then suddenly he told me that he was going on a mission to Washington and proposed to take me with him. This was baffling but exciting. Next he indicated that the mission would have something to do with shipping, and possibly oil, and that Lord Leathers, who was then Minister of Shipping, would probably be of the party. I could not help asking myself why, if the Minister was going, there was any need to send Beaverbrook as well. Perhaps as a sort of Churchill spy? And what about the leadership of the House of Lords? It was all very mysterious. Soon afterwards came news from Robertson, the General Manager of the *Daily Express*. We were to go by train to Prestwick in Scotland, thence to fly across the Atlantic. I was to hold myself in instant readiness; the whole thing was a deep secret, my parents would be informed as soon as I was safely in America. Curiouser and curiouser – the whole affair was beginning to resemble Alice in Wonderland.

Curiouser yet, one lunchtime I was given by Robertson a special pass and told that at one o'clock the next morning a car would call for me at my Knightsbridge flat and take me to Olympia railway station. Why on earth this little used station in the inner suburbs, when there were plenty of trains from Euston whence passengers for the West of Scotland normally departed? Punctually at one o'clock a uniformed chauffeur presented himself at my door. We proceeded westwards to Olympia. The station was, of course, shrouded in black-out. Shadowy figures inspected my pass and I was led to an obviously predestined place on the platform. Presently a long train steamed slowly into the station. It seemed excessive as I recalled that, so far as I knew, its only passengers would be Beaverbrook, Nockels, myself and possibly Lord Leathers. A door was opened, and I stepped into an open coach filled to my astonishment with recumbent members of the Royal Marine Corps. Stumbling past and across them I passed into the corridor of a sleeping-car coach. The first door was labelled, as I recall, Major-General Jacob – then Sir Alan Brooke, Chief of the Imperial General Staff – Lord Louis Mountbatten – Mr Martin (Churchill's chief private secretary) – the Prime Minister – Lord Beaverbrook – and, the first door of the next coach, Mr Farrer. As I stepped nervously, exhaustedly, into my compartment I was dimly aware that I seemed to have become a supernumary in an extremely high-powered mission.

By daylight, as we rolled through the Midlands, Beaverbrook confirmed this fact. 'Are we all going to fly?' I asked stupidly.

'No, Queen Mary.'

My first idiotic reaction to this news was that I had brought no warm clothes suitable for a sea voyage. I asked him what role he was going to play. He was evasive and grumpy. 'That fellow Churchill made me come.' In fact, I discovered, the journey had been arranged, on the Prime Minister's initiative, at very short notice. Its main purpose, in his eyes, was to counter the growing insistence of the American Admiral King that the Pacific was the most important theatre of war. He was taking all his big guns with him – and Beaverbrook too, for he was well aware of his influence with Roosevelt and his top civilian advisers.

Late that afternoon we arrived at the quayside at Greenock. There in the roadstead lay the giant liner, RMS Queen Mary. She had been lying there for four days. Her numerous passengers, who included the King of Norway, had been chafing at the delay; they were further disgruntled when they were moved into more cramped quarters, leaving the most comfortable part of the ship for the mission. I was to live, during the voyage, in quarters far above my station.

It was a most pleasant voyage, marred only by one fact. Nockels is by constitution incapable of even seeing a ship with-

out feeling sea-sick. As soon as we boarded the Queen Mary
he retired, green at the gills, to his cabin and was seen no more.
As, for nine days, we pursued our ziz-zag course at thirty knots
across the Atlantic I had to be valet as well as secretary. Secre-
tarial duties, however, were light, Beaverbrook spent long hours
closeted with Churchill. I did however – ominous sign – have to
prepare a private memorandum about the Second Front. I
frequented the Promenade Bar, made friends with the barman,
who was thrilled at the thought of serving the greatest in the
land. Fourteen years later I returned in the Queen Mary from
New York. After I had ordered my second drink the barman
leant across the counter and said: 'Excuse me, Sir, but weren't
you with Mr Churchill's party in 1943?' Even royalty could
not have done better.

Two days out from Staten Island, where for security's sake,
to avoid the inevitable publicity of New York, we were to
land, we were given our disembarkation orders. The mission was
divided into three parts, the great ones, the not so great, and
the *hoi polloi*, but for additional security disembarkation and
the ensuing motor-cavalcade to the railway station were to take
place in reverse order, the *hoi polloi* first, the great ones last.
The former duly disembarked, unaware that the news of the
mission's arrival had leaked, but not of its reverse order. Crowds
lined the route to the station, waiting to cheer Churchill, and
naturally they started to cheer the first car that appeared. This
car contained, inter alia, Nockels and myself. Rising to the
occasion we each leaned out of a window, acknowledged the
plaudits and gave the V sign. At least both sides of the street
thought they had seen the great man. We were travelling too
fast for them to detect the impostures. It was a delectable
moment for us both.

In Washington the Beaverbrook party was accommodated at
the Wardman Park Hotel, some way from the Pentagon and
White House. This suited Beaverbrook The further away the
better, for he wanted to participate as little as possible in these
particular Anglo-American discussions. His position was anyway difficult; he was neither an official member of the mission –
nor a Cabinet Minister. His hope was to confine himself to

unofficial discussions with both Churchill and Roosevelt, but
singly, not together. Over the Pacific he could back the Prime
Minister to the hilt, but it was soon obvious that other subjects
would come up for discussion, and above all the question of
what to do about Russia and her attitude to Poland. About the
Poles Beaverbrook cared very little, Churchill very much,
Roosevelt, so Beaverbrook told me, inclined more to Beaverbrook's attitude. The best way, in Beaverbrook's view, to give
succour to Poland was to establish an immediate Second Front.
Once we had satisfied Stalin's constant demands we should be
in a far stronger position. Roosevelt – again Beaverbrook was
my source of information – was strongly inclined to agree, to
be prepared in fact to trade the Pacific for the Second Front. A
confrontation seemed to be looming up – Churchill versus the
President and Beaverbrook.

To be fair, though he made a good deal of mischief during his
stay in Washington, Beaverbrook did do his best to avoid this
particular confrontation. On the first weekend in Washington
he received an invitation from Roosevelt to spend the Saturday
and Sunday at one of his hideouts; Churchill was to be the only
other guest. Beaverbrook told me to telephone to Harry
Hopkins saying he would prefer to be excused, he was sure
Hopkins and the President would understand. Hopkins's reply
was sharp and instant. 'Tell Lord Beaverbrook,' he snapped at
me down the telephone, 'that the President is not accustomed
to having his invitations refused.' Even Queen Victoria could
not have been more regal. Beaverbrook went.

He went again a little later in much happier circumstances.
The mission had departed and Beaverbrook had stayed behind.
Thomson always maintained that he only joined the mission as
an excuse for an American holiday. In this he was for once
unfair, but a holiday Beaverbrook did now take. As for
Churchill he returned to London with the assurance that
Europe would remain America's chief concern, but he had got no
satisfaction over the Poles, and a Second Front that year was
still an open question. The mission had been a qualified success,
Beaverbrook had done little to ensure anything better. I could

not help wondering whether the leadership of the House of Lords would be open to him when he returned.

The second visit with Roosevelt began on the Friday the mission left. Beaverbrook himself described to me how it started. The President, he explained, had the greatest admiration for Churchill as a great war leader, but on occasions he found him an unconscionable bore; the fellow would never for one instant stop talking, pontificating, about the war. Not even at meal times, not even over brandy and cigars. Now, having bid his demanding guest farewell, Roosevelt settled with an audible sigh of relief into his compartment on the Presidential train. He was carrying a large portfolio which he proceeded to open. For a moment Beaverbrook was afraid he might be in for a discussion of war aims or the plight of the Poles. But no. 'Now,' said the President, 'that Winston has gone, I can get down to my stamp album again.'

While the cat was away the mice arranged for a little play. Beaverbrook had told us he would be back on Monday morning. I went to stay with a friend in a house in the grounds of Dumbarton Oaks, of which cultural appanage of Harvard he was deputy-curator. There I played bridge for stakes which I fondly imagined were fifty cents a hundred, only to find, after I had won, that they were fifty cents – a point. Nockels on the Sunday was to be fêted, wined and dined by members of the Federal Bureau of Investigation with whom he had hobnobbed during the first Washington conference after Pearl Harbour. Some premonition made me return to the hotel before dinner on Sunday evening. About nine o'clock I heard a voice crying in the passage, 'Nockels, Nockels', followed by the slamming of a door. I went into his room to find a Beaverbrook on the rampage. 'Nockels, where the hell is the damn fellow?' It was impossible to cover up for him. 'I'm afraid he's not in yet, Sir.'

'I want a bath, I want my pyjamas, where are my pills?'

I did my best to soothe the angered breast. I ran the bath. I laid out the pyjamas. I found the pills. I hovered round, metaphorically tucking him up as an Edwardian nanny would tuck up her fractious charge. Presently I was dismissed, and returned to the room I shared with Nockels, to await the return of my errant friend. It was about two hours later that I heard the well-known voice approaching down the passage. 'Tra-la-la, tra-la-lee,' it warbled, 'Tra-la-lee, Tra-la-lo, tra-la-la' – the door was flung open, and he stood framed in it. 'California here I come,' he sang, and did a little jig as he approached my bed. 'Dear boy,' he chortled, 'it's been wonderful.' I paused a moment for effect, then 'Nockels,' I said, 'he's back.' For a second it failed to register, then his face turned ashen. Caught in mid-jig, he cried in anguish 'Oh my dear Lord.'

He was punished of course. He was told that he must find his own way to New York, whither we were now bound, by train and by the cheapest class. Beaverbrook and I were flying. The punishment fell, however, just as much on my innocent head. When we arrived at the Waldorf Towers there was of course no Nockels. I had to do all the unpacking. Anyway, as so often he rose magnificently above it all. Perhaps I helped by elaborating the whole incident to Beaverbrook and making him laugh. He was very fond of his inimitable valet, whose passport incidentally was now marked 'Personal Secretary'. Very soon the old commanding presence was re-established. 'Nockels, where are my shoes?'

'Beside your dressing table, my Lord, where you always like them.'

Nockels was the hero of another incident on this trip. We went to stay with Beaverbrook's old Canadian friend Jack Bickell, of blessed MAP memory. Bickell lived in an astonishing mansion about twelve miles west of Toronto; it was about a hundred yards long and one room wide. A bachelor, he and his house were run and dominated by a she-dragon of a house-keeper whose word was apparently law. This she-dragon had no doubts about the proper place for such a humble member of the human species as a personal secretary; the answer was 'below stairs'. I found myself allotted a bedroom in the basement and a place at table in the servants' hall.

I was inclined, at least temporarily, to shrug the whole thing off, but Nockels flew into a rage on my behalf. First he insisted on himself serving me my meal in the bedroom. Next he announced that he would go at once to lodge a vigorous protest with our master. 'Oh, Nockels,' I said, 'let it be. I couldn't really care less.' (This wasn't strictly true, I cared quite a lot!) He was adamant, and the next morning Beaverbrook said to me:

'What's all this Nockels tells me?'

'I'm quite comfortable down below.'

'God damn it, if Bickell doesn't change the arrangements I'll tell him we're leaving at once.'

Rejoicing inwardly at the approaching discomfiture of the she-dragon I replied falsely: 'I really shouldn't bother.' I knew that he would bother, and he did bother. I emerged into the upper air and took my place in the dining room.

Our stay chez Bickell was anyway to be short. Beaverbrook grew quickly bored with his old friend, and even more with the old friend's friends who were asked to meet him. After forty-eight hours I was told to invent a telephone call from Harry Hopkins summoning him back to Washington. We caught the midnight sleeper-express and got off next morning in New York.

During the days that followed before we left for England he was at his most benign. I was allowed several evenings off. For one of them he got me the 'house' seats for what had just become the smash-hit Broadway musical of all time. I must have been one of the first Englishmen to see Oklahoma, only three weeks after its opening. Not to be outdone, Nockels wangled matinée seats a little later. Beaverbrook loved New York – it is arguable that he was always more at home there than in London – and on this occasion he was far from averse to the adulation and entertainment offered him by his newspaper and other friends. I never heard a word about shipping or oil. For a brief space the war, for the three of us in the Waldorf Towers, seemed hardly to exist. His only worry, it seemed, was how to avoid the Duke of Windsor.

We were sandwiched, in this luxurious skyscraper apartment block, between the Duke and his Duchess two floors above and Madame Chiang-Kai-Shek two floors below. Madame made no approaches, but the Duke made many. Languishing now far away from the battle lines as Governor-General of the Bahamas, he was most anxious to talk to his old friend and adviser who

in the fateful days at the end of 1936 had fought so hard to
preserve him his throne. Beaverbrook was well aware what the
Duke wanted; in his search for a more important job, he would
ask Beaverbrook to act as intermediary for him with his other
former fierce champion who was now Prime Minister. Beaverbrook was determined to do no such thing and extremely
anxious to avoid having to tell the Duke so to his face. He was
constantly 'out for a walk' when the Duke telephoned. Finally
however, he was driven into a corner; he could not be that
rude. He told me to telephone the Duke's equerry and fix a time
when he could call on him. I asked for the Duke's room and
when a male voice answered, said in my most Oxford voice:
'Can I speak to the equerry to his Royal Highness?'

'The Duke speaking,' came the reply. I lost my head completely, said 'Oh God' and put the receiver down. Beaverbrook
who had been listening, was paradoxically furious. 'What the
hell do you think you're doing, speaking to the Duke like that?'
For the rest of the day I was in disgrace. There was a streak of
snobbery in the self-proclaimed man of the people.

By modern standards our flight back to England was uneventful. Today I find flying the most boring form of transportation
imaginable, but in 1943, it still had a spice of adventure about it.
Very few people, after all, had so far done it, across the Atlantic,
and even wastelands like Gander and Goose Bay, those Newfoundland staging posts, spelled a sort of romance. At Gander
indeed we stopped, and there I presented my 'short snorter' for
signature by fellow-traveller Averell Harriman and others.*
Also waiting at Gander on another flight was the comedian Bob
Hope. He and Beaverbrook eyed each other, I thought, somewhat askance. There was a further short stop, once more at
Foynes, with breakfast at the Adare Arms, and then we were
home once more.

Home for me, and I think for Beaverbrook too, proved a sad

* A 'short snorter' was a dollar bill which, once countersigned by a
bona fide flyer of the Atlantic, certified that you had flown it too.
It was much prized and flaunted at the time.

letdown. Great events were obviously pending, but for the moment the war seemed to be marking time. The Sicilian landings, the Russian summer offensive, were still at the blueprint stage. And when these great events, of which he had full foreknowledge, did materialize, what part, if any, would Beaverbrook play in them? Would the summons from No. 10 to rejoin the Government be repeated? There was no sign of it. Had his behaviour in Washington put paid to his chances? It looked like it. He was sick and tired by now of doing nothing. There were still his newspapers, but the salt of Fleet Street had lost much of its savour. One morning, about two months after we had returned to England, we were driving up from Cherkley to London. Suddenly he turned to me. 'Farrer,' he said, 'Churchill has been a great war Prime Minister. He saved the country. But now he should go; he's outlived his usefulness. What we want now is a Prime Minister who can make peace.' I made some sort of protestation and he dropped the subject. But what did this remarkable pronouncement portend? Had the great supporter of the Second Front — 'Strike out, strike now' — suddenly reverted to the old pre-war appeaser? Or was he again wearing the phantom crown? Was *he* the man who would lead the country safely on the paths of peace? Or was it just the random utterance of a man whose every nerve tingled with frustration? His mind was never easy to read. Perhaps at that time he really was indulging in a pipe dream. In any case I did not need to worry, for I knew by then that at a word from Churchill the dream would vanish and 'like an insubstantial pageant faded, leave not a wrack behind'.

LORD PRIVY SEAL

SUMMER MERGED into autumn, and still Beaverbrook was lurking in the wilderness. I drafted his letters, wrote some articles for his newspapers, most of which were Beaverbrook-inspired, impassioned pleas for a Second Front. Visitors to Cherkley came and went. On the field of battle the Russians were surging forward, the Anglo-Americans had landed on the Italian mainland, the Japanese tide was at last ebbing. But on the Surrey Hills and at Brook House, Park Lane, we were in the doldrums. Those months were for me the most disheartening of the whole war. Then, without warning so far as I was concerned, a fresh wind blew up and filled our sails. In October Lord Beaverbrook rejoined the Government – but without a seat in the War Cabinet – as Lord Privy Seal.

So the caravan was reassembled and pitched its tents in what proved to be its final resting place, the stately Georgian mansion of Gwydyr House in Whitehall, just opposite the Horse Guards Parade. But one of its members was very nearly left behind.

Within hours of his appointment I got wind of a rumour that only Thomson was to accompany him. Nockels confirmed this. In desperation I took drastic action. George was told to be at Gwydyr House at a certain hour on a certain morning. With his full collusion and though I had had no instructions, I went too. Presently, apprised of my presence, the new Lord Privy Seal sent for me.

'What are you doing here?'

'I'm working for you, Sir.'

'God damn it, who told you to come?'

'Thomson told me he was coming, so – '

'I told Thomson, I never told you.'

Silence. Then: 'Don't you want to go and work for the *Daily Express?*'

'I'd much rather be working here – with you.'

He looked at me searchingly, then: 'Now you're here, you'd better stay.' Thankfully I went upstairs to the top floor room which for nearly two years was to be Thomson's and my abode.

The staff at Gwydyr House was small. It consisted of the two personal secretaries, Peter Masefield, and Miss Hogg, together with assorted secretaries and typists. Peter Masefield,* a leading air correspondent, joined us shortly after Beaverbrook's appointment, as his unofficial adviser on civil aviation, one of the subjects the Lord Privy Seal had been given to tackle. Miss Hogg was the only true civil servant among us, ruler of the Private Office. What her initial reactions were to us visitors from outer space she never revealed, but friendly relations, as on previous occasions, were soon established. She had, at first meeting, a somewhat forbidding mien, sturdy, fair-complexioned, spectacled. She adopted it, I suspect, deliberately. It was her first experience as head of a Private Office and Beaverbrook was, to put it mildly, a Minister outside her previous ken. She soon, however, had him under control; where Miss Hogg was concerned he was normally as good as gold.

A frequenter of Gwydyr House was Armorel Dunne, who had waved Nockels and me goodbye at Waterloo on my first trip to America. She was now personal driver to 'C', the thinly anonymous head of MI6, and as such paid almost daily visits, bearing secret documents which she would hand to Miss Hogg, thereafter ascending to pay a courtesy call on Thomson and myself. On one occasion she found our room empty, our desks strewn carelessly with papers. At that time the famous humorous columnist 'Beachcomber' was running a mock spy story with a *femme fatale* spy called Dingi-Poos as its chief character. When we returned to the room we found, scrawled in lipstick across our papers, the legend 'Dingi-Poos has been here'.

Beaverbrook was as good as gold in the Cabinet too. There

---

* He is now Chairman of the British Airports Authority.

were no frictions with colleagues. Perhaps this was because he had no department for which to make exorbitant demands. With Churchill his relations were of the most harmonious kind. The Second Front, long a subject of controversy, had now been agreed. He was in a sense the odd job man of the Government, but this did not mean that his influence in Cabinet was negligible. Though not a member of the War Cabinet he was almost always summoned to attend it. His advice, on such matters as post-war foreign and economic policies, was powerfully given, frequently heeded. It was in a way for him a halycon period, free from the stresses of 1940 and 1941. It was a time too when his relations with the Labour ministers grew closer than before. In particular was this the case with the Home Secretary, Herbert Morrison. It became a custom for Beaverbrook to ask Morrison and Brendan Bracken to dine with him every Monday evening after the afternoon Cabinet meeting. Indeed, if he had not issued the invitation by Monday morning, Morrison would unfailingly ring up either Thomson or myself to enquire if he were expected. Bracken did not bother, he could blow in whenever he liked.

Soon after Beaverbrook's appointment Churchill was off, via Cairo, to the first great tripartite conference at Teheran. Shortly before he had attended the funeral of the First Sea Lord, the titular head of the British Navy, Admiral of the Fleet Sir Dudley Pound. Together, from our top floor window, Thomson and I watched the procession as it marched, to the Dead March in Saul, down Whitehall from Admiralty House towards Westminster Abbey. At its head, immediately following the gun-carriage, walked the Prime Minister. We noticed his curious gait, the left foot shooting out now and again almost at right angles and the fact that all the time he was losing distance from the gun-carriage. In retrospect, was this the first small sign that this giant of a man, now in his late sixties and carrying a burden unparallelled in British history, was beginning in health, if nothing else, to falter? It occurred to neither Thomson nor myself for a moment; we had a suspicion that he might perhaps have lunched rather too well, that was all. Nor when, visiting North Africa on his return from Teheran, he was taken seriously ill, did the public think – they dared not think – that this might be the beginning of the end. Only a very small inner circle were afraid. Their spokesman was his personal physician, Sir Charles Wilson.* Any ordinary man, he told Mrs Churchill and the Cabinet, would need to lay off for at least six months after such an attack of pneumonia. Churchill decided to lay off for just about three weeks. For his convalescence he was lent by the Americans the famous Villa Taylor in the Southern Moroccan beauty spot of Marrakesh.

To Marrakesh, in the last days of 1943, he summoned Beaverbrook to be adviser-confidant in residence, and to Marrakesh the Lord Privy Seal flew, dragging with him a very reluctant personal secretary.

My reluctance was due to purely selfish reasons. I was informed of my journey precisely three hours before his Lordship was due to set out. This gave me no time to alter or cancel engagements, above all to warn an old friend whom I had not seen since the war that I could not after all have him to stay. Even a year earlier I should not have let these considerations weigh with me. But the war had been going on a long time and the end still seemed a long way off; among civilians in particular I think war weariness was damping down the ardent flame of patriotism. Anyway this particular little cog in the war machine was furious at this interference with his private affairs, and I had long since discovered the best way of indicating to Beaverbrook my displeasure: I sulked. He could sulk himself on occasions, but sulkiness in others to his face baffled him. All the way to Lyneham airport (some ninety miles) I sat withdrawn in my corner of the car. At dinner en route at an hotel in Marlborough I answered his questions monosyllabically. In the plane I composed myself at once for sleep, leaving Nockels to shoulder the burden. Earlier in my career with him I would not have dared to behave in such a way; now I am ashamed of having done so. How misguided my attitude was is shown by the following letter I wrote to Thomson a week later.

* Very shortly to be Lord Moran, and author of the highly controversial book *Winston Churchill: The Struggle for Survival*, London, 1968.

5 January 1966   *In North Africa*

MY DEAR GEORGE,

The sun shines continuously, the scenery is all that could be desired, and it is hard, nay impossible, to keep to my resolution of sulking.

Everything is provided in the most lavish manner and without any charge, cars are laid on, beakers of brandy, eggs, oranges.

The Master is, or was yesterday, ill with temperature and bad tummy ache. He was convinced he was (a) dying and (b) being killed by Lord Moran. But Nockels has just telephoned to say he is better this morning.

I live in a hotel; Nockels to his chagrin has to share a room where the party is staying.

There will be much to tell you when I return, which should, I think, be soon.

Yours ever,
David.

It was from his shared room in the Villa Taylor (my anonymous hotel was the Mamounia) that Nockels greeted General Eisenhower. Churchill's method of convalescing was to spend hour after hour in conference with all the big wigs of the North African campaign. Biggest of all the wigs was General Dwight D. Eisenhower, the Allied Commander-in-Chief. (He had on two occasions, I think, visited Cherkley.) He was due one morning at a time when I was waiting in Nockels's room to be summoned by our Master. The room gave on to the main courtyard of the villa. Presently we heard martial noises outside, the shouted command, the stamp of Spahi boots, the presenting of arms. Then the great man himself appeared at the courtyard's entrance, walked slowly along towards where we waited. Everywhere the military saluted, the civilians stood stiffly at attention. He reached our open window, and suddenly I heard the familiar voice beside me saying, with a beautiful blend of welcome and condescension: 'How *are* we, Sir, how *nice* to see you again!'

That same evening, Beaverbrook was involved in an embarras-

sing contretemps. Churchill asked him to dinner to meet the
French General Georges, throughout the war a staunch opponent of Vichy France and in 1940 overall commander of the
British forces at the time of Dunkirk. Beaverbrook got the time
wrong and arrived half an hour early. The General too was
over-punctual. He was ushered into the room where Beaverbrook was waiting, the two men were introduced and left alone
together. There followed, Beaverbrook told me afterwards, a
long embarrassed silence. Unhappily the Lord Privy Seal spoke
no French, M. le Général had not a word of English at his
command. It needed the arrival of their host, with his fractured
but fluent French, to break the ice.

The farewell party, given two days before our departure by,
I think, the French Naval Attaché in the villa, provided in its
way a sequel. I arrived early and found myself in conversation
with my host, two other Frenchmen and Lady Diana Cooper.*
The talk was in French. Presently Beaverbrook entered the room
and made towards our group – Lady Diana was one of his oldest
friends. Then he heard the alien tongue. He hesitated, he
hovered – a thing I had never seen him do before. I went on
talking. Then at last Lady Diana espied him. 'Max,' she cried,
'come and join us.' Rather sheepishly Beaverbrook did so. We
then discovered that both the Frenchmen spoke fluent English,
and all was well.

The following morning Beaverbrook said to me: 'Tell me
Farrer, how long would it take a man of my age to learn
French?'

Meanwhile, at the Mamounia Hotel, I basked in the winter sunshine, ate breakfast among the orange and lemon trees in the
garden, went on at least one expedition into the foothills of the
Atlas Mountains. There had been a muddle on our arrival. Max
Aitken had travelled with his father from London, and was to
spend two nights in Marrakesh en route for Cairo where he was
to take up a new appointment as Group Commander. A room

* Her husband, Duff Cooper, was at that time British Ambassador to
the Free French in Algiers.

was available for him, none had been booked for me. Diffidently it was suggested to him by the British colonel who was in charge of the hotel's security and other arrangements, that we might share. No one could have blamed him for consigning his father's junior personal secretary to a mattress in the corridor. Instead we spent what to me were two delightful days together, at times pulling his father and my employer affectionately to pieces. And I inherited his room.

Marrakesh was for me an almost complete holiday. I saw my master only in the mornings – it was twenty minutes by car from the hotel to the villa. Anyway he was borne off usually in the afternoons by Churchill on sketching or sight-seeing expeditions, suffering, so he told me, agonies of boredom. It was at Marrakesh that he first got to know General Montgomery, for whom he soon formed a large admiration. It was perhaps natural that these two arch-individualists should take to each other, but the victor of El Alamein had with my master something else in common. Socially neither of them came out of the top drawer. It was as natural in fact for Beaverbrook to prefer Montgomery the soldier to General Alexander (the other hero of North Africa) the Guards officer as it was for him to get greater pleasure from the company of Mrs Wallis Simpson than from that of England's Queen.

Soon we were on our way home, with Churchill allegedly fully restored to health. We flew to Gibraltar where then as now the process of landing convinces me first that we are going to plunge into the Straits of Gibraltar, and a moment later that, having landed we are going straight into the Mediterranean at the other end of the runway. Thence, to my excitement and, it was to prove, my subsequent acute discomfort, we embarked in the largest battleship afloat, HMS King George v. On board I was assigned to what was grandly termed the Admiral's spare cabin. I was unaware that the Admiral inhabited this large and commodious room only when the ship was in port. It lay immediately above the great ship's twin screw; in motion the vibration was unspeakable. The marine who looked after me was sympathetic, but there was nothing he could do. I spent four totally sleepless nights. On the second day out, somewhere off the coast of Portugal, we had what was called a practice 'shoot'. I was cordially invited to attend. I was, it was true, warned to put cotton wool in my ears and cling on to the rails. The noise and the blast, as the great ship's eight sixteen-pounders fired their salvos at their imaginary target, were like nothing I have heard before or since. If, I thought later, my mastoid ear has survived this, I really ought to be in the army.

In due course we reached Plymouth, and thence by special train, Paddington. My baggage now included two large wicker baskets, full of forbidden fruit. 'Oranges and lemons, cried the bells of St Clements,' and it was oranges and lemons, unobtainable in Britain throughout the war, which in the succeeding days became almost the staple diet of my friends.

Beaverbrook, shortly after his return from Marrakesh, had to take up his appointed task of dealing with the international aspects of civil aviation. The Prime Minister detailed him to be Britain's representative in the forthcoming negotiations with the Americans on this complicated post-war subject. At first he welcomed this new, concrete task. Soon however his secretaries were aware that it bored him; it bristled with abstruse problems such as overflying, domestic as against international routes, a mysterious thing called 'cabotage'. Moreover it was a subject on which the Americans held all the aces and were pressing for a conference in Washington. Lastly it concerned solely the post-war period. Beaverbrook saw little honour or glory, even in the unlikely event of *successful* negotiations. He began to try to pass the buck. Let the Foreign Office take over, he advised Churchill, or Lord Leathers or Lord Woolton – though why either the Ministers of Shipping or Food, anyway fully occupied already with the affairs of their respective departments, should be better equipped than he to deal with the problem, he never explained. Anyway he could not avoid the preliminary discussions already arranged in London on the subject between himself and Adolf Berle, one of the American under-secretaries of State.

At this stage, on the eve of Berle's arrival, Thomson gave

himself unnecessary trouble. He sent Beaverbrook what was intended as a jocular memorandum, informing him that Mr Berle's main interest in life was the Tractarian Movement. At once the Lord Privy Seal was on the telephone from Cherkley in a state of considerable excitement. Who *were* the Tractarians? Patiently Thomson explained to this man who boasted of his Presbyterian ancestry and who was over-fond of quoting the Old Testament, that the Tractarians were a group of clerics who, in the previous century, were in revolt against the current attitudes of the Church of England. Among them, said Thomson, was a man called Newman who had 'gone over' to the Church of Rome, become a Cardinal and had written a famous book *Apologia Pro Vita Sua*.

'Ah! Cardinal Newman, go and buy that fellow Berle a Cardinal's hat, buy it quickly.'

In the event Thomson managed to get hold of a first edition of Newman's *Apologia*. On his return from this shopping expedition George remarked to me sadly, succinctly: 'Quite mad, poor gentleman.'

Adolf Berle came and went, and nothing was decided. Later, however, in a speech in the House of Lords, describing the field of civil aviation, the Lord Privy Seal caused a minor sensation. 'Cabotage,' he declaimed in his strong Canadian accent, 'is one of the problems we have to face.' Several elderly peers reached nervously for their hearing aids. 'What does he say, what does he say?' they chorused. 'Cabotage' Beaverbrook repeated, 'is one of the – '

'Sabotage!' cried their elderly Lordships, 'Disgraceful, disgraceful, shame!'

Increasingly the British and American governments were concerning themselves with the problems of post-war reconstructions. In retrospect this seems as far-sighted as it was optimistic. The war was far from won. The Second Front had yet to be attempted, and already there were ugly tales about of a new German secret weapon. In the autumn of 1943 the RAF had spotted some mysterious installations at Peenemunde in East

Prussia. They were adjudged by the experts to be launching sites for a new giant rocket. Was it to be the Blitz all over again? Beaverbrook took a gloomy view, sharing the view of a section of the Cabinet that the attack would be launched early in 1944. The moment passed, but Beaverbrook's fears persisted. In a memorandum to the Prime Minister he advised widespread reorganizations of the Home Front to meet the new peril, dispersal of factories, etc., etc. His memorandum was not acted upon.

In the international field, post-war problems depended, it was clear to all concerned, in the last resort on the behaviour of Joseph Stalin. In the eighteen months before the end of the war in Europe Churchill's and Roosevelt's attitude to the Russian dictator were widely to diverge, with results disastrous for Europe. In the meanwhile Beaverbrook gave me the recent cables exchanged between the three men, and told me to digest them for his benefit. It was thus that I learned that Roosevelt and Churchill always referred to Stalin as 'Uncle Joe'. This nickname was the key to a remarkable conversation between the Prime Minister and the Lord Privy Seal which shortly afterwards I overheard.

I must explain that, as secretaries to a Cabinet Minister, Thomson and I had a button attached to our telephone extensions which when pressed down 'scrambled' the conversation of the two speakers so that it was unintelligible to anyone trying to tap it. Secretaries, once they had scrambled, were supposed to refrain from listening in.*

One morning, in the earlier editions of the *Evening Standard*, there appeared a cartoon by Low which was highly unflattering to the Prime Minister. Beaverbrook was nervous and felt guiltily responsible – unnecessarily, since he had not been shown it in advance, and after all he was always telling fellow Ministers that he never interfered with his newspapers. But still – On that same morning, unknown to him, Churchill had received a particularly insulting cable from Stalin. About

---

* Each Minister had his own secret telephone, already 'scrambled', on which he could talk direct. Painted green, these telephones were known as the 'green line'.

three o'clock in the afternoon one of Churchill's private secretaries came on the phone. 'Is your master in?'

'Yes, just back from lunch.'

'The Prime Minister wants to speak with him. Will you scramble?'

I pressed the button, and I am afraid remained with my ears glued to the receiver. The following conversation then took place.

Churchill	(in rich post-prandial voice): Max, that fellow Uncle Joe –
Beaverbrook	(on tenterhooks and mishearing): Don't worry, Prime Minister, don't worry.
Churchill	What are we going to do about him? He's sent me –
Beaverbrook	(interrupting): Don't worry. I'll sack him tomorrow morning.
Churchill	What are you saying?
Beaverbrook	I'll sack him. He shall never appear in my newspapers again.
Churchill	What are you talking about? I said Uncle Joe.
Beaverbrook	(after a pregnant pause, flatly): Oh!

Increasingly in those days I was being given by Beaverbrook the task of digesting the memoranda to the Cabinet which arrived in their little red boxes in an unceasing flow on the Lord Privy Seal's desk. Normally they proved turgid reading, reflecting little credit on the Ministers or their amanuenses who compiled them. Too often they said in four pages what could easily be said in one. They showed little improvement on a document presented by Neville Chamberlain in the urgent summer of 1940 which concluded: 'It is the opinion of my committee that a further investigation should be undertaken, taking into consideration all those matters of which in the opinion of the new committee, consideration should be taken.'

In contrast, one series of weekly despatches brought a breath

of fresh air into this documentary world.* They came from our
Washington Embassy: they were signed 'Halifax'; it was an
open secret that the author was the Ambassador's press attaché,
Isaiah Berlin. These despatches should be published in full, in
book form. One in particular I recall. It recorded how when
General de Gaulle was paying his first official visit to Washington, it was decided that the new French hero should pay a
courtesy visit to the veteran and aged American soldier who
had commanded the American troops on French soil in World
War I. De Gaulle and General Pershing were duly introduced.
'Ah yes,' mused the old soldier, 'tell me now, how is my old
friend Pétain getting on?' De Gaulle rose to the occasion.
'Actually,' he replied, 'I haven't seen him for some time.'

The winter passed slowly, the spring more slowly still. In May
we had a mild diversion at Gwydyr House. A telegram came
from Adolf Berle, saying how pleased the US Senate had been
about Beaverbrook's statement on bases. Statement? What
statement? Beaverbrook was puzzled, anxious. He consulted
Thomson, Peter Masefield, me. Statement? It must refer to his
recent 'cabotage' speech in the House of Lords. But he had said
nothing about bases. Hansard was consulted. Then rather slyly
I suggested that Berle might be referring to something said in
conversation. 'Oh,' said Beaverbrook, 'plenty was said in *conversation*: of course we'd be prepared to trade bases for aircraft.' What price the British Empire? But the incident was
forgotten, swallowed up in greater events that were pending.
  Increasingly the broad shadow of that pregnant woman, the
Second Front, was covering all our lives. We all knew now that
it was coming. But when and where? To a very few the secret
was known and meant to be known. I was not of their number.
To some of the little red despatch boxes I was not allowed
access. It is, however, sometimes possible to put two and two —

  * Beaverbrook's own memoranda was another exception. These, however, I did not have to digest. He had all too often shortened my original
draft.

or in this case one and one – together and get the correct answer. Through my hands, early that spring, passed a memorandum from the Minister of Transport concerned with the movement of trains and other vehicles. Shortly afterwards I read a memorandum from the War Office dealing with leave for the troops. The two fitted like the missing pieces in a jigsaw puzzle. I was reasonably certain, within a fortnight, when, but not where, the Second Front would be launched. And so, when very early in the morning of 6 June 1944 I heard streams of aircraft passing overhead, I was able to say to my brother, who came to breakfast once a week with me after his fire-watching stint at his office: 'Leslie, this is D-day.'

This was the day for which Beaverbrook had been impatiently waiting for more than two years, the day for which he had been almost prepared to risk his friendship with Churchill. Yet once it had arrived, he showed curiously little excitement, remarkably little tension about its outcome. He was not directly concerned in the conduct of the Normandy landings or in the subsequent Anglo-American offensive. Tension came to Gwydyr House not on 6 June but about ten days later with the advent of the flying bomb.

Of the prospect of a new German secret weapon I had been fully apprised. There had been little attempt at secrecy about it in Governmental circles, though views on what form it would take varied sharply. A rocket, an unmanned aircraft? For at least four months its arrival had been daily awaited. It made its debut by night. The air-raid warning sounded, and the inhabitants of the block of flats where I lived congregated on the first-floor landing which, for some unexplained reason, we considered the safest place in the building. It was however far from sound-proof. Very soon there came that high-pitched whine, with which we were to become depressingly familiar and, some little time after, silence followed by the noise of the explosion. 'That' I said to my companions boastfully and drawing a bow somewhat at a venture, 'is Germany's secret weapon.' I was right.

The flying-bombs proved to have no more than a nuisance value. But they were launched at a time when the public's nervous reserves were low, and Britain had been for a long time largely free from bombs of any kind. 'Oh God!' was the feeling, 'not all over again.' Moreover they gave the most unpleasant warning of their approach. One heard them coming. At least a normal bomb, and later the rocket, took one by surprise. Paradoxically too the public found it more difficult to take this new assault when victory seemed just round the corner than they had the Blitz when they were fighting for their existence. Beaverbrook shared the public reaction in exaggerated form. He conjured up a nightmare of factories in flames, production disrupted, our armies starved of weapons, thrown back into the sea. He pressed upon the Prime Minister, the War Cabinet, in even more urgent terms than previously, the need for dispersal and other measures to meet this new and dangerous crisis. He was rightly ignored. Within six weeks the German launching sites in the Pas de Calais had been overrun. Did he really believe in this crisis he had conjured up? Though he was never two-faced, there were often two faces to this remarkable man. I think he convinced himself that the country was faced by a new emergency. I think too he saw in it the opportunity to play a principle role once more. For if this was a new time of crisis, who better to cope with it than the old trouble-shooter of 1940-1?

It was not to be. Instead Churchill sent him to Washington to discuss the problem of post-war supplies of oil. Initially I was to accompany him, but then I discovered that the civil service was to be represented on this mission by my old friend Victor Butler, who was then Assistant Secretary at the Ministry of Fuel and Power. Immediately I feared for that friendship. Among the maxims that had on occasions a strong appeal to my master was 'Divide and Rule'. I had seen it in operation before. I could hear him now saying: 'God damn it, that fellow Butler, what's he been up to? Find out what he's thinking, get him to tell you his Minister's instructions.' I did not put it beyond him to tell the said Butler some purely imaginary criticisms I had made of him. I told Beaverbrook that I thought Thomson knew far more about the oil situation than I and with that white lie secured my exclusion from the journey.

In point of fact, neither Thomson nor I knew anything about it at all.

The journey justified my apprehensions. In Washington Thomson and Butler were allotted a joint double room in the Mayflower Hotel. Having discovered this, Beaverbrook told Thomson he must find himself separate accommodation. In the same circumstances I would have meekly yielded. Thomson was made of sterner stuff. Having already struck up a close working relationship with his civil service vis-à-vis he stoutly refused to budge.

The journey was also fruitless. In the circumstances it was bound to be, unless the mission had been led by a Minister already reconciled to post-war American dominance. Beaverbrook was not such a man.

The season of post-war planning was at hand; Adolf Berle's civil aviation discussions in London had been its herald. This planning was designedly, by both sides, based on the Anglo-American alliance of which Beaverbrook was a firm supporter, but increasingly throughout 1944 and into 1945 he came to see, as many of his colleagues did not, that the Americans were bent on playing the role of spider to Britain's fly. He struggled very hard not to walk into the American parlour. Wherever possible he stonewalled, gaining nothing but giving nothing away. To this extent his visit to Washington in July 1944 might be held to have been a success; nothing was accomplished but nothing yielded. But it was very like procrastination in the hope of a later miracle. America's economic power was as great as Britain's indebtedness. There was a parallel in the fighting in France. British and American forces had landed in Normandy in approximately equal strength. Two months later the balance in favour of the Americans was nearly two to one.

So Beaverbrook returned to London increasingly aware, I believe, of the amalgam of admiration, pity and ruthlessness with which the American Administration, and in particular President Roosevelt, now regarded their ally. His links with individual members of that Administration however remained close, his affection for Roosevelt undimmed, his friendships with his newspaper friends unaffected. Among these was the

famous Claire Boothe Luce, dramatist, columnist and recently
elected a member of Congress. Mrs Luce was due to arrive in
London to stay with Beaverbrook in his Arlington House flat.
Nockels was given strict instructions. 'Remember, she's a
Congresswoman. When she arrives you say "Good morning,
Congresswoman".' The aristocrat in Nockels was silently in
arms. 'Yes, my Lord,' he replied meekly but decided otherwise.
I was not present at the Congresswoman's arrival, but I am
quite sure Nockels greeted her thus: 'Good morning, Mrs Luce,
how nice to see you.'

One morning in the autumn of 1944 Beaverbrook handed me
at Gwydyr House a lengthy Cabinet document and told me to
give him a précis. It was an account of the talks known as the
Bretton Woods discussions that had been taking place in
America about the post-war funding of Britain's enormous
Lend-Lease debts. Its author was the British delegation's leader,
the ex-Bloomsbury grouper who had become a world-famous
economist, Maynard Keynes. I spent a fascinating day reading,
marking and, I really believed, inwardly digesting this remarkable document. My knowledge of economics was, and is, shaky
in the extreme, but such was the skill of this very brilliant man
in marshalling arguments, the wit with which he presented
them, the lucidity of his style, that the whole thing seemed to
me as clear as daylight. I was bedazzled into thinking that
Keynes's proposals were totally acceptable. I said as much to
Beaverbrook when I gave him my précis. He read it, then
turned to the document itself. Having scanned it, he rebuked
me sharply. 'Farrer, if the Government accept these proposals
it will be the *ruin* of the British Empire.'

Briefly, what Keynes was proposing was a massive, long-term
American loan, with many strings attached, to tide Britain over
her early peace-time problems and to maintain the parity of the
pound sterling. At once all Beaverbrook's suspicions of
American intentions, that had been aroused during his recent
Washington visit, crystallized into certainties. Accept the
Bretton Woods proposals, he told me, and you condemn Britain
to economic vassalage. Far better to reject them, however harsh
the post-war privations which the British people would have

to endure. Under Churchill's leadership they would accept and survive them, whether he led a coalition government or a Tory administration voted into power on the strength of his popularity at a general election. But for one gigantic miscalculation, he may have been right; his reasoning depended entirely on his conviction that the country would confirm Churchill in power. The post-war story of Britain, without Churchill, staggering from one economic crisis to another makes sorry reading. In any event, in the following year Beaverbrook opposed Keynes tooth and nail at every opportunity, in Cabinet, in the House of Lords, in conversation with Churchill. In Cabinet he became the leader of the minority which was finally overthrown, in the House of Lords he was a voice crying in a wilderness of incomprehension, from Churchill he extracted a measure of sympathy. An appeal to patriotism, to the future of the Empire, could always rouse an echo in the Prime Minister's heart. But his sights were set now on two targets only, the winning of the war and the post-war containment of Russia. He was largely oblivious of domestic problems, of, for example, the fact that the acceptance of Sir William Beveridge's report on the future of the social services ensured for Britain at least a semi-socialist society in the post-war years. In those closing months of World War II Churchill was far less a contemporary man than his old Canadian friend who saw clearly what was likely to happen, and hated what he saw.

As the year 1945 approached the mood in Britain was buoyant. Victory was certain, and soon. The flying-bomb menace had been curtailed, our 'gallant' Russian allies were 'liberating' huge tracts of Eastern Europe and the Anglo-Americans had liberated the whole of France. Despite minor setbacks, all seemed set fair. Beaverbrook did not share this general optimism. Britain was certainly winning the war and, in his view, almost as certainly pursuing policies which would lead to her losing the peace. His mood was sombre. But on New Year's Eve at Cherkley he cast his cares aside. He entertained a festive gathering ushering in the year of victory. I cannot recall in detail the guest list. It almost certainly included his son Max and his daughter Janet, Lord Castlerosse, old colleagues like

Patrick Hennessy and Archie Rowlands, Michael Foot, Brendan Bracken, a sprinkling of ladies. It certainly included Mr A. V. Alexander, the Socialist who held the post of First Lord of the Admiralty. Early in the proceedings Beaverbrook had to answer the 'green line' telephone, on which Ministers and high officials could communicate secretly with each other. Thereafter there was dinner, *Destry Rides Again*, and more drinks in the big drawing room. Midnight and 'Auld Lang Syne' were approaching when the door was thrown open to reveal Nockels, weaving slightly. 'Beg pardon,' he announced in trumpet tones, 'but the green Lord is wanted on the first line.'

II

VICTORY AND DEFEAT

IT WAS towards the end of 1944 that Churchill, discussing with Beaverbrook the political situation after the war, indulged himself in a pipe dream. Should he, he asked his companion, resign his leadership of the Tory party and appeal to the country as a purely national figure. Beaverbrook's reply was this: 'If that flock of asses and mules are deprived of your leadership they will wander into strange pastures.' His dislike of official Toryism dated from the day in 1922 when Stanley Baldwin became Prime Minister. It never really abated. His real friends among the Tory leaders were maverick individualists like Brendan Bracken and Colonel Moore-Brabazon, one of his successors at the Ministry of Aircraft Production – and of course Churchill, the greatest maverick of them all. If he could have chosen Churchill's cabinet for him, it would have been a motley crew, certainly including the above-named, with Herbert Morrison, his Monday evening dinner guest and Nockels's 'Green Lord' from the Labour benches, outsiders like W. J. Brown, the independent member for Rugby; some of his favourite industrialists like Patrick Hennessy and possibly Trevor Westbrook, Peter Masefield in charge of Civil Aviation, possibly, who knows? George Malcolm Thomson, elevated to the peerage, as Lord Privy Seal. It would have had a short life but probably a merry one. He knew however that, pre-eminent as he was, Churchill in a peace-time election would be chained to the Tory machine's chariot wheels. The Conservative Central Office would take over.

Beaverbrook discussed with Thomson and me the chances of the Labour Party remaining in the coalition after victory in Europe had been won for the period, then estimated at two

years, it would take to defeat Japan. Beaverbrook thought that
Attlee and his colleagues might be satisfied if they were given
all the twenty-five constituencies which the Coalition had won
in wartime by-elections. Thomson and I contested this. I think
I suggested that they might be satisfied if the Tories surrendered
to them seventy-five seats, which would bring them up to near
parity with their former and future opponents when full peace
was restored. The conversation seemed to me anyway
extremely hypothetical. It was hard to believe, after so much
frustration, so many setbacks, that victory was really so near.
Hitler's talk of a new secret weapon was not *all* the boasting of
a frightened man. The rockets (V2s) which had started to fall
haphazardly and in small numbers on Britain, were capable of
inflicting great damage. The German offensive in the Ardennes
seemed for a few days to threaten the Allied lines of communication to the sea. The Rhine was uncrossed, in Italy the
Germans held firm on the Gothic Line. Besides, even if victory
in Europe did come in the spring or summer, I believed that
Clement Attlee, who had been an exceptionally loyal and
successful Deputy Prime Minister throughout the war, would
persuade his Party to soldier on *without* an election till Japan
was defeated.

Meanwhile preparations were going forward for the new
meeting of Roosevelt, Churchill and Stalin which was to take
place at Yalta in the Crimea. Beaverbrook, Stalin's great friend,
was not to be included in the British party. Though he never
told me so I think he was bitterly disappointed. Could his
presence at the Conference have made the slightest difference?
Stalin might well have been pleased to see him; after all, in the
autumn of 1941 he had helped the Russian dictator to get a
good deal more than Churchill had intended. But the answer is
no. What was agreed and minuted at Yalta provided the basis
for a perfectly reasonable post-war settlement of Europe. It was
solely because of the way the Russians interpreted those agreements that the Iron Curtain was so soon to drop.

So Beaverbrook was left behind. His odd jobs had been
accumulating. He had been appointed Chairman of a Cabinet
committee on housing, he still dabbled in oil, still concerned

himself with civil aviation. Above all he was pre-occupied with his struggle with Maynard Keynes. Without this fight on his hands he might, I think, have again resigned. Yet in Cabinet discussions his was still the sharpest mind of them all. He pleaded his special causes – independence of American aid had now taken the place of the Second Front – powerfully and sometimes deviously. He had his own ways of trying to win friends and influence people. With Churchill he did not need to use them. The Prime Minister received from him a greater comradeship and stimulus than from any other colleague.

Meanwhile in Gwydyr House I was occupied in drafting memoranda about the Lord Privy Seal's various odd jobs, in making précis of the leading articles in all the newspapers and of the various Cabinet documents which Miss Hogg extracted from the red despatch boxes. There were always too his letters to attend to and write for him. By this time he seldom did more than glance at what I had written. I had acquired the Beaverbrook style which I have never wholly lost. On one occasion our joint failure to read over what I had written nearly caused acute embarrassment. The son of a fellow Cabinet Minister had been reported missing in the Burmese jungles. Beaverbrook told me to write a letter of condolence to the Minister's wife. I drafted it and gave it to a typist who placed it on Beaverbrook's desk. It ended – or should have ended – 'I do want you to know how much I feel for you at this time.' Sometime later I noticed the letter lying on the dispatch desk, duly signed by Beaverbrook. I glanced at it, then snatched it from the desk. In transcription the second 'e' in 'feel' had become 'l'.

The months before the end of the war in Europe were, for me personally a time of almost continual misjudgements. I believed that the Coalition Government could be maintained, or that if not the Tories would win the election. I maintained that the Yalta Conference had been a success, suffering still from the pro-Russian virus with which Beaverbrook had injected me three years earlier. I considered that the death of Roosevelt was a shattering disaster, not only in itself but in the light of the

apparent nonentity from the Middle West who would succeed
him. 'I'm just mild about Harry' was the current American
quip; I subscribed to it. In the event the Coalition split asunder,
and Labour won the ensuing election with the second largest
majority of the century. The Russians broke all their promises.
In the following years Harry S. Truman proved himself an outstanding President. His idea of Marshall Aid was a turning point
in post-war history. I was not alone, however, in these misjudgements. They were all shared to the full by the man for
whom I worked. Beaverbrook was never a good prophet.

The Anglo-Americans crossed the Rhine and advanced deep into
Germany; the Russians were approaching Berlin; in Italy
General Alexander's forces had broken into the valley of the
river Po. Hitler was dead. At last it was all over bar the actual
signing of the instruments of unconditional surrender. VE day
was at hand, and indeed was unofficially announced for 5 May.
Then there was a hiatus, curiously parallel to the two-day delay
at the beginning of September 1939 before Britain officially
declared war.* There was a hitch over who would sign where.
Finally on 7 May at Rheims the Germans signed in the presence
of American, British, French and Russian witnesses the document of unconditional surrender. It was all over. The lights
came on again in the London streets. Huge crowds gathered in
front of Buckingham Palace to cheer the Royal Family and the
Prime Minister. A few days later came the victory parade.
Beaverbrook threw Gwydyr House open to friends of all who
worked there. We had in fact front-row stalls, but even as the
first detachments marched past us down Whitehall the rain
began to fall. It continued to fall throughout the day. The
victory fireworks that night were almost drenched in rain. Were
the skies weeping at the prospect of Britain's sad post-war
decline?
      After the victory? It soon became clear that Churchill's

* The Germans invaded Poland in the early hours of September 1st.
Britain declared war at eleven a.m. on September 3rd.

hopes of a continuing Coalition running a National Government were to be dashed. Had Attlee, or Herbert Morrison, or Ernest Bevin, had even Aneurin Bevan known that the defeat of Japan would take not two years but two months, the Coalition might have lasted. 'Nye' Bevan was the chief architect of Labour's victory. Few if any of the Labour Ministers who had served under Churchill – many of them for over five years – really believed that he could be defeated at the polls; but outside the charmed Ministerial circle Bevan had his ear far closer to the electoral ground. He predicted not just a narrow victory for Labour but a resounding triumph.

So the Labour Ministers resigned, and Churchill set about forming a Caretaker Government to prepare the country for the first General Election in ten years. Beaverbrook was asked to remain as Lord Privy Seal. He demurred vigorously, he would be far more useful conducting his newspapers in support of the Conservative cause. But the Prime Minister needed him at his side as his chief adviser on electoral strategy. Outside the Government he might, with his known dislike of official Conservatism, do more harm than good. He persisted in his request which was almost a command. A bargain was struck. Beaverbrook would remain in office, but Churchill would allow him to resign the moment the election had been won.

Once committed, Beaverbrook plunged into the fray with typical forcefulness and élan. Dropped now was all pretence that as a Minister he took no part in the conduct of his newspapers. He master-minded their every story, their every leading article, their every fresh attack on those opponents who had so recently been Beaverbrook's colleagues. He plunged too himself directly into the fray in support of his friend. He contracted to speak in support of Conservative candidates, at Chatham, at Ashton-under-Lyne, at Worcester. You could almost hear the echo of his Second Front speech in New York. 'Strike out for Russia, strike now,' but this time it was 'Strike out for Churchill, our great leader, strike out *against* the Socialists, those misguided men who would turn this land of free men into a police state' (I am, of course, paraphrasing, but the words are very similar to those which he dictated to me for a newspaper article not long after the Labour Government took office.)

It was heady stuff. It was also tactically disastrous. There was a case for exalting the man whom on the day of his death President de Gaulle, no particular friend, was to call 'le Grand Churchill'. Beaverbrook was shrewd enough to realize that but for Churchill's immense prestige the Tories were unlikely to win, but to attack and vilify men who had taken their full part in the war effort was a major blunder, infuriating their normal supporters and alienating large sections of the floating vote. Not for the first time Beaverbrook in the weeks after VE day was largely out of touch with public opinion. The workers at the factory benches, the members of the armed forces, the air-raid wardens and the fire-watchers (those unsung heroes) look-ed forward to the new and better Britain they had so often been told they were fighting for, and which had to some extent been foreshadowed in the Beveridge Report. How could they expect the Tories, who had been in power all through the thirties, that period of mass unemployment, hunger marchers and the dole, to provide it? There was a far better chance with men like Attlee, Bevin, the ex-docker, Morrison, the policeman's son. The more Beaverbrook attacked them, and persuaded Churchill to attack them, the more their supporters, actual and potential, rallied to their side.

I am writing from hindsight, and looking back it is clear that a different tactic from Beaverbrook's might have lessened, but could not have averted, the Tory defeat. I was, and remained for another year, very much under my master's spell. I voiced no criticism of what he was doing. After all, during the election campaign, crowds turned out in their thousands to cheer Churchill to the echo whenever he appeared. Ought we at Gwydyr House, ought the denizens of the Tory Central Office, to have realised that what these crowds were saying was not 'You have led us to victory in war, now lead us to victory in peace,' but 'Well done, God bless you, and *goodbye.*' Lloyd George in 1918 had gained his Pyrrhic victory in his Khaki Election. Times had changed in 1945.

Beaverbrook's first personal foray into the electoral field

proved to be a disaster strongly flavoured with farce. In the Caretaker Government Brendan Bracken held the post of First Lord
of the Admiralty. Now he was candidate for the overwhelm-
ingly naval constituency of Chatham and Rochester. So far as I
know Bracken had few connections with the sea, he had
certainly never been a sailor. Nor, for that matter, had his
predecessor. Beaverbrook spoke for him at his first election
meeting. 'Brendan Bracken,' he exclaimed to a packed audience,
'will be the greatest First Lord of the Admiralty since Nelson.'
The catcalls, whistles and laughter that greeted this astonishing
comparison were echoed next morning in all save the Beaverbrook newspapers; if indeed comparison it could be called, for
Nelson had never been first Lord of the Admiralty. In due course
Bracken went down to defeat. For a time there was a coolness
between the two men.

I and Nockels accompanied the Lord Privy Seal northwards
for a temporary stay in Manchester's Midland Hotel. He was to
speak for the Tory candidate in neighbouring Ashton-under-
Lyne. It was the same constituency which he had himself
represented when he was a Member of the House of Commons
from 1910-17. When Lloyd George formed his first Coalition
Government at the end of 1916 he at first told Sir Max Aitken
that he would be in the Cabinet. In those days elevation to
Cabinet rank involved fighting a by-election. Aitken told the
local Tory leaders at Ashton that a by-election was likely
shortly. Then Lloyd George changed his mind. Face had to be
saved. A peerage was the only answer, for a peerage would also
involve a by-election. So Aitken became Baron Beaverbrook.*
Such is the story as he told it to me. Now he was returning to his
old stamping ground.

I accompanied him to the election meeting in this, one of the
dingiest of all Lancastrian towns. He was on edge as we drove
out from Manchester, the Chatham fiasco rankled, but he was
encouraged by the fact that only a few days earlier Churchill
had received a rapturous reception from a huge crowd in a
neighbouring town. His own reception might be described as

* He told me once that it was the worst decision he had ever made.

fair to stormy. He had his supporters, he had his hecklers. His speech was carefully prepared. It contained no gaffes, it was largely a panegyric on Churchill, but I could not rate it a success, and the congratulations showered on him by the candidate and his chief supporters seemed to me to have undertones of doubt if not of desperation. It was then that I myself felt the first twinges of doubt about who would win.

I did not go with him to his meeting at Worcester, where the sitting member had a five-figure majority. I was left behind in the Queen's Hotel in Birmingham to sample again how extraordinarily disorganized at that time English provincial hotels could be. But I had helped to prepare the speech. It was part praise of Churchill, part virulent attacks on Labour leaders, the left-wing head of the London School of Economics, Professor Harold Laski, being now a special target.* When later the election results were declared the Tory member had got in by four votes.

By the end of June it was all over bar the counting. But this took three weeks while from all over the world the votes of the Forces were coming 'express' to be added to the ballot papers of those at home; they amounted to 10 per cent of the total vote. July 19 was the appointed day. I was on holiday that day in Cornwall. The first result was expected about eleven in the morning. The solidly bourgeois inhabitants of the Ferry Boat Inn, Tory supporters all, gathered round the wireless in the lounge, all prepared to be jubilant. At first the results came slowly, then gathering in momentum. By lunch the omens were plain even for those uninitiated in the mysteries of electoral swings to see. The meal was eaten in gloom that bordered on despair; there was even dark talk of communism stalking the land, and when I ventured the thought that Stalin would probably much prefer to negotiate with Churchill than with Attlee nobody would listen. By mid-afternoon there could be no last lingering doubt; for the first time in history we were to have a Socialist Government with a clear majority over all the other parties.

* The *Daily Express* had begun to build this figure from the groves of Academe into a sort of communist bogeyman.

For me the result presented no personal problem. This had been posed six weeks before. I felt certain then that, however much a freshly elected Churchill pleaded, Beaverbrook would in no circumstances join a new Government. My days in Whitehall were over. I had taken stock of my position. This time the alternatives seemed to me to become a fully-fledged journalist with one or more of his newspapers or to become a sort of personal attendant. The latter appealed at the time more than the former. It would mean variety, travel abroad, and I knew that I was reasonably secure in his affections, for I had overheard him six months previously instructing George Millar (his man of affairs) to include me in his will. 'But, Sir,' Millar had protested, 'you only do that when they've been with you ten years.' 'To hell with that, put him in now.'

All the same, hadn't the time come to break away? I had been with him for more than five years. During all that time there had been scarcely a dull moment. I had been stimulated, excited, amused, angered, overworked. I had learned a great deal, and above all I had been privileged to work with an outstanding man at the apex of his career. But working with him at close quarters had the effect of taking constant overdoses of pep pills. In the summer of 1945 the inevitable reaction had set in. Probably only the fact that while he was still a Minister I still felt at the centre of things had prevented it doing so earlier.

So I made plans to escape. I consulted an old friend of my brother who held a high position in the BBC. He told me there would shortly be a vacancy in Paris for an assistant to the Corporation's chief correspondent. If I liked to apply he would talk to the Director-General, Sir William Haley. I duly did so, very considerably exaggerating my command of the French language, and then went on holiday to Cornwall. When I returned I awaited nervously and expectantly the hoped-for summons. In due course it arrived and I presented myself before Sir William. He cross-questioned me briefly, though he made no attempt to probe my French. Then he asked me my existing salary which I told him. He paused not quite long enough, then he said: 'I'm sorry, Mr Farrer, we can't offer you the job. It carries a lower salary than yours, and it's against our principles to offer a man a lower wage than he has been getting.' It was so obviously a way of saying I wasn't fit for the post. I am sure the phrasing was kindly meant, however, insincere, but for the moment it humiliated me and a little later it enraged me. It still rankles. Years later I met Sir William, by that time Editor of *The Times*, at a dinner party. He became involved in an argument about the family name of a certain peer and about whether he was the third or fourth holder of the title. Our host had to fetch *Who's Who* from upstairs to resolve the argument. It was another guest who whispered all too audibly : '*The Times* ought to know top people by heart, without having to consult *Who's Who*.'

12

THE FINAL YEAR

So THE escape route was closed. Luckily Beaverbrook never knew that I had attempted it. I had much anyway to be thankful for. Working for him might be exasperating, nerve-racking at times, but it was never dull, and now that he was freed from the almost intolerable burden of collaborating with colleagues of equal or even superior rank, now that he had become again dictator of his own newspaper empire, perhaps the pressure would slacken. Anyway my salary was now four times what it had been before I joined him, and this at a time when cantering, if not galloping, inflation was still in the future.

I had thought that the alternatives now would be Fleet Street or Personal Attendant; Beaverbrook decided on an amalgam of the two. I was to spend a lot of time with him at Cherkley or Arlington House, but I shared with Thomson an office in the steel and chromium Daily Express building and before long I was writing a weekly political article in the *Evening Standard*. It appeared each Tuesday. On the previous day it was vetted, altered, amended, often cut by Beaverbrook. Increasingly, as I grew more practised, the style, the allusions, the comparisons were mine, but the opinions remained those of my master.

After the atom bomb had destroyed Hiroshima (and had led immediately to the Japanese surrender) nothing could ever be the same on the international scene. On a far lesser scale, after the Labour Party's victory at the polls, the same was true of Britain's domestic politics. Beaverbrook seemed largely oblivious of both these facts. Re-reading my articles of this time, I find that not one of them touched, except obliquely, on international affairs. Perhaps this is understandable. The policies of the new Foreign Secretary, Ernest Bevin, were calculated to enrage any left-wing Socialist and to bring comfort to any Tory. Bevin was a Socialist, and an old enemy of Beaverbrook too, but the latter could not help but applaud the way the former defended British interests and beat the Commonwealth drum (to Beaverbrook it always remained the Empire). He could not bring himself to praise, but he refrained from blame. But on the home front he bent his, and my, every effort to trying to put the clock back. 'Attack' was his motto; attack everything the Socialists were trying to do, attack the Health Service, Nationalization, raise the Communist bogey in the shape of the politically inept, if economically brilliant Professor Harold Laski, attack the Tories whenever he felt *they* were not attacking enough. It made for pungent, hard-hitting journalism; it seems in the light of events curiously old-fashioned. For good or ill a semi-Socialist state – and Keynes's American loan which was its main buttress – had come to stay. Beaverbrook had been defeated and could not admit it.

I attacked the Bretton Woods agreements in an article headlined 'Worse? No. It was better after 1918', claiming that 'to accept these proposals would mean that we should have to reduce the standard of living in this country for a generation.' I attacked the Labour left-wing as represented by Professor Laski and his followers in an article headlined 'There's a Caucus Close Behind Us' (I was rather fond of the title), in which I accused them of trying to push Attlee and Bevin into disastrous pro-Russian policies (the Beaverbrook-Stalin honeymoon was over). There was an article headlined 'Strait Jacket For You', in which I attacked those Conservatives who thought 'that the only way back to power is to show the country that modern Conservatism is really only Socialism writ smaller'. In 'The Mantle of Elijah' I mused upon a likely successor to Churchill as Tory leader, coming up with such rather unlikely successors as Sir David Maxwell Fyfe and Mr Manningham Buller, both of whom were later kicked upstairs to the position of Lord Chancellor, who politically has very little influence of any kind. In fact Farrer-Beaverbrook in those three months of autumn and winter struck out right and left, to no other purpose than to restore a state of affairs which could never be restored. 'Free Enterprise' we cried,

and we may have been right. 'Down with economic serfdom to
the United States,' and again there is a case for the slogan. But
it was not the time effectively to proclaim it.

Perhaps it was this yearning for the remembrance of things
past that prompted Beaverbrook that autumn to pay his first
post-war visit to Paris. He wanted also to make contact with old
French newspaper friends. Among them was Jean Provoust,
famous editor of *Paris Soir*. On the eve of the French collapse in
1940 Provoust had sent Beaverbrook a telegram: 'Help us to
help ourselves.' He meant, send us all your aircraft. Beaverbrook had, to his enormous credit, with the backing of Sir
Hugh Dowding, refused to do any such thing. Since then
Provoust during the 'occupation' had somehow managed to
survive. He was back in the saddle, where at an advanced age
he still remains.

Paris was not a success. It may have been free, it was very far
from gay. Austerity stalked its streets, stalked even the corridors
of the Ritz. It was the coffee served by that famous and august
hotel that after a very few days drove Beaverbrook back to
London. It was made from the grounds not of the coffee bean
but of the hazel nut. Back in England his restlessness at this
time was shown in his more than usually compulsive interference with his editors. I would sit with him for anything up
to an hour and a half at Cherkley while on the telephone he
praised, blamed, criticized, harangued, bullied his editors. Even
George Malcolm Thomson, now chief leader writer for the
Daily Express and book reviewer for the *Evening Standard*, was
not wholly immune, though he was never bullied. George could
have remained in Government employ. The Civil Service was
indeed more than anxious to claim him for their own; he had
opted for his old master, preferring perhaps the extremely
engaging devil he knew . . .

At the *Daily Express* Christiansen still reigned supreme, as did
John Gordon at the *Sunday Express*, where he continued to pon-
tificate weekly. He was assisted as news editor by Harold
Keeble who possessed an unrivalled flair for the good news story,
and in due course succeeded Gordon. At the *Evening Standard*
the brilliance of Frank Owen and later of Michael Foot had been

replaced by the more pedestrian qualities of Herbert Gunn. This
rather unlikely father of the poet Thom Gunn was a superb
technician and under his guidance the *Evening Standard*
achieved an immense competence, but competence was not
what Beaverbrook really wanted from his favourite brain-child.
He required from it not dividends but prestige. He delighted in
the fact that in many circles it was still known as the 'West-End
Parish Magazine'. Gunn became the butt of his fiercest and
frequently unfair sallies. Finally he failed to stay the pace.

These were the men with whom I now came in contact, with
whom I drank in Fleet Street pubs often to the detriment of
my liver, and who made my life far more pleasant than I had
anticipated. They might have looked on me with some suspicion
as a possible spy for their and my Lord and Master; they were
far too generous-minded to do anything of the sort. It was the
aim and ambition of every young journalist from the provinces
seeking fame and fortune in the big city, to be taken on by one
of Beaverbrook's newspapers. The editors of these newspapers,
aided by the Beaverbrook magic, were, in those days, the
reason.

Meanwhile, usually at Cherkley now, the greatest journalist
of them all was in an unsettled mood. He was kicking not only
against the political but the social pricks as well. It is very rare
for a man who has held high political office not to miss it once
it is no longer within his grasp. Beaverbrook was no exception,
and he knew that he would never regain it. He knew too that
the 'good old days' would never return. To him those days
socially meant all those goings on so faithfully chronicled in
Valentine Castlerosse's 'Londoner's Log'. They meant supper
parties for Gertrude Lawrence after her latest first night, 'routs'
at Stornoway House, the brief excitement of the reign of King
Edward VIII, the world described in Sir Henry Channon's
Diaries. It would be grossly unfair to compare the worlds of
Beaverbrook and 'Chipps', self-confessed in his diaries as a
social butterfly of an engaging but particularly futile kind, but
the events and milieu described by the latter had played a considerable part in the leisure moments of the former. Now those
relatively carefree and, for the rich, sunny days had gone for-

ever. When in 1939 Beaverbrook was shouting 'There will be no war' he was meaning 'There *must* be no war', for he knew, as Neville Chamberlain knew at Munich, that the world he had known in the decades after 1918, and helped to fashion, however successful the war's outcome, would vanish forever if it took place.

Perhaps, however, it had not vanished across the Atlantic. Very early in the new year of 1946 he decided to pay a visit to New York and thence to the sunshine of Bermuda.

Early in February 1946 my mother died. My devotion to her had been total. As soon as he was given this news Beaverbrook telephoned to me to sympathize and to tell me to take a fortnight's holiday. During this period he wrote to *ask* me if I would like to go to Bermuda with him. I accepted with alacrity. Had I refused I am sure it would have made no difference to our relationship. He could be totally sensitive and sympathetic to those who worked for him when they were unhappy and in trouble. So travellers' cheques were provided, visas obtained. We were off again, Beaverbrook, Nockels and I.

The start of each of the four main journeys I made with him were fraught with the unexpected. In 1942 there had been the reserved aircraft which proved to be teeming with passengers; in 1943 there had been the mystery departure from Olympia in the Prime Minister's special train; in 1944 I had been required to depart for Morocco, sulking, at three hours' notice. Now in 1946 the departure of Nockels and myself for New York had an unexpected prelude in a three-day stay at a seaside resort.

It had been a bitterly cold winter, and light snow was falling as our train left Waterloo Station for Bournemouth, whence we were to find our way to Hern Airport, some ten miles distant. (Beaverbrook was to drive there direct from Cherkley.) At Bournemouth it was snowing heavily, and we were told that the airport was closed down. We were taken for the night to a hotel somewhere in the hinterland of this favourite holiday venue for middle-aged Midlanders who yearly travelled there in the Pines Express from Manchester and Birmingham. Having unpacked for the night we went in search of a much-needed drink, only to find that it was a temperance hotel.

At least one other New York-bound passenger was in pursuit of the same stimulant and received the same dusty answer. She introduced herself as Thelma Furness. Nockels rose at once to the occasion. 'My dear Lady Furness, do allow us the privilege of taking you somewhere where we can eat *and* drink.' She accepted with but a trace of surprise, we sallied forth into the blizzard and Nockels led us unerringly to a bar-restaurant.

Before the evening was over it was clear that Lady Furness was fascinated by Nockels. He behaved quite beautifully, ordering an expensive wine as to the manner born, flattering her, solicitous for her every wish. She was clearly at a loss as to how to place him, she also clearly delighted in his company. His courtliness was positively old-world. He made no attempt to place himself; nor did I, but I was very much the junior partner, Nockels was in control. As the blizzard continued for the next forty-eight hours she proved a fascinating companion.

Thelma Lady Furness, a sister of Gloria Vanderbilt, had been in the late twenties and early thirties one of London Society's leading beauties; she still in the mid-forties had immense chic. She had also been one of the closest friends of the Prince of Wales, his constant companion at his Surrey home of Fort Belvedere. On one occasion she had to be away for six months in the United States. Before she left she decided to introduce the Prince to her closest friend, a woman called Mrs Edward Simpson. She had hoped, she told us, that Mrs Simpson would 'keep her place warm for her'. On her return to England the friendship of the two women came to an abrupt end, and Fort Belvedere knew Lady Furness no more. But she bore no grudge against the Duke of Windsor. He was, she told me, one of the most delightful companions she had ever known.

At last the blizzard stopped. Over icy roads we skidded our way to the airport. There, awaiting us impatiently, was Lord Beaverbrook. He and Lady Furness were old friends, but for a moment he was otherwise preoccupied. 'Nockels,' he shouted, 'you packed both my mufflers.' Nockels slipped automatically into the role of gentleman's gentleman, fussed solicitously, and

I suppose a little guiltily, round his master and, so far as I recollect, gave him his own scarf to wear. I do not know who was the more surprised, Lady Furness at the metamorphosis of Nockels and the realization of who we were, or Beaverbrook as he watched his personal secretary escorting his old friend solicitously towards the aircraft, carrying her rug over my arm. Later, after we had settled into the aircraft, he was a little tetchy about the whole incident.

Our stay in New York was uneventful, our journey to Bermuda was not. Beaverbrook was stopping off at Washington en route, to visit old friends, to refresh himself perhaps with a nostalgic whiff of wartime days. He decided to leave Nockels and me behind to find our own way direct. Unlike those far off days of 1942, this time we made no demur, we would have two free days in New York. One of Beaverbrook's American friends put his private Grumman aircraft, complete with pilot, at our disposal, in which to fly down to Baltimore where we could board a flying boat for Bermuda.

It was wet and very windy when we arrived at La Guardia Airport, and the aircraft looked very small. Illogically I am more scared in a small plane or a small ship than in their larger sisters. As regards ships I have a valid excuse: I am usually sea-sick in anything smaller than twenty thousand tons. With planes I tell myself vainly that there is more chance of coming out alive after a forced landing in a twin-engined four-seater than there will be if a jumbo jet goes wrong. To no avail, the smaller the means of travel, the more I am frightened. We boarded the Grumman and took off safely. I endeavoured to compose myself for sleep, and succeeded in dozing fitfully. Waking from one of these dozes I saw in front of me in the aircraft a very familiar figure. It was Nockels, at the controls. Immediately, it seemed to me, the aircraft was wobbling dangerously, side-slipping, about to perform a probably fatal loop-the-loop. It was, of course, pure illusion. We were holding a perfectly steady course, and after we had landed – the pilot once again at the controls – Nockels was congratulated on being

an exceptionally apt pupil. Nonetheless I felt distinctly queasy
as we booked in for the night at one of Baltimore's hotels.

By midnight I was feeling not queasy but violently ill. Victor
Butler, now in his last weeks as petroleum attaché at our
Washington Embassy, had travelled forty miles to dine with
me at Baltimore's allegedly best fish restaurant. There I had
eaten bad crawfish. Solicitously Nockels sat by my bedside for
half the night while I retched, shivered and finally sweated the
poison out. During the four hours flight the next day in the
Bermuda-bound flying boat I made a slow recovery. We landed
safely just across the harbour from Hamilton, Bermuda's
capital. There followed an apparently endless muddle and
delay over customs and immigration, after which BOAC mis-
laid its launch. It was three hours before at last we reached
Hamilton. Then there was an hour's journey by horse-drawn
vehicle before we reached the cottage which Beaverbrook had
been lent. It was a very bedraggled personal secretary who
greeted him. Beaverbrook took pity on me and sent me to bed.

Next day I told him in detail the saga of the voyage. He told
me to write an article about it. I did my best to be savagely
satirical about the muddle I had experienced. Beaverbrook
approved it, told me to cable it in full to the *Daily Express*. The
next thing was an enraged protest from the BOAC representative in Hamilton, to whom the cable operator had apparently
shown the article. At first Beaverbrook stuck to my guns, but
later he decided not to offend the organization which after all
would have to fly him home to London. I cabled Christiansen,
telling him not to publish.

'Cottage' our temporary residence was called, but by English
standards it was a sizeable mansion. It nestled prettily below
the famous Mid-Ocean Golf Club – with a view across a bay to
the American base loaned to the United States early in the war
in exchange for fifty largely obsolete destroyers. Here we ate,
bathed, did a little work. It seemed to me that Beaverbrook
was more nearly relaxed than at any time I had known him. He
even complimented me on my swimming, surprisingly since it
consisted solely of a rather maidenly breast stroke, head held
as high as possible out of the water. But he did not forget his

newspapers. At least three times a week he was talking to one or other of his editors on the transatlantic telephone.

One day he took me with him on a shopping expedition to Hamilton. Except for the Governor's car all civilian motor vehicles were then still banned in Bermuda. We jogged peacefully in our 'Surrey with the Fringe on Top' along the island's oleander-fringed roads. We were walking down Hamilton's main street when suddenly there hove in view a flamboyant figure, panama-hatted, striped-trousered, walking with an exaggeratedly rolling gait. He stopped in front of us, threw out his arms, exclaimed: 'Lord Beaverbrook. This is a real pleasure.' It was immediately obvious to me that my master hadn't the faintest idea who this apparition was. The same realization dawned simultaneously on Mr X.

'The name is Glancy,' he added, somewhat apologetically.

'Ah! Yes,' Beaverbrook replied, while I turned away, choking with suppressed laughter. Very soon Mr Glancy proceeded on his way, somewhat subdued. Beaverbrook turned on me rather querously. 'What's the joke?'

'Don't you remember?'

'No.'

So I told him.

One Sunday morning, perhaps three years earlier, Beaverbrook had telephoned to me at my flat. 'Take a cable to –' I couldn't catch the name. I asked him to repeat it. Still I couldn't get it. Once again I asked for a repeat. It was no good. Finally I had to ask him to spell the name. There was a brief pause, then:

G – for God Almighty
L – for Lunatic
A – for Atlantic Ocean
N – for Nancy
C – for Cunt, and
Y – for You.

Then in an ever rising crescendo of annoyance: 'Now have you got it?'

'Yes, Sir. It's a pity there isn't a B in the word.'

When I had finished the story Beaverbrook said: 'God, Farrer, did I really say that? I'd forgotten.'

During these comparatively halcyon, and as it turned out penultimate days of my official association with him, there was one row over which I was far more to blame than he. Beaverbrook had as house guests Sir Alexander Korda and Pamela Churchill, the estranged wife of Randolph. He gave a dinner party for them. Nockels and I occupied a bungalow, separated from the main house by a courtyard. At about seven o'clock Nockels told me that I was not to be included; we were to dine apart, *à deux*. 'My dear boy, it's monstrous, but there it is.' I was quite unreasonably angry. There was no reason why he should invite me to his dinner party if he didn't want to. Perhaps the memory of my night in the servants' hall chez Bickell had left its mark. I told Nockels that if later in the evening Beaverbrook called me on the house telephone he was to answer that I had gone out for a walk. 'But, dear boy, it's deluging with rain.'

'That's the whole point.'

He did telephone and the point was taken. Next morning Beaverbrook told me it was all a misunderstanding, 'due to that damn fellow Nockels'. This was grossly unfair, but it served its purpose. It was a victory rather meanly won. I would never have fought the battle had I not known that once again an escape route lay open.

With the death of my mother I had inherited money – enough, I thought at the time, to make me independent. My future colleagues in the publishing world, Fred Warburg and Roger Senhouse, had for some time been urging me to join them and put capital into their firm which, on a flood tide of success, they wanted to expand. Negotiations were proceeding and were in an advanced state. I could contemplate with a degree of equanimity the prospect of leaving my exacting, fascinating, bewildering employer. It was in this mood that I told him shortly afterwards that I had to return to England to help wind up my mother's estate. He made no objection and I felt correspondingly guilty; there was no need for my presence in London, my brother had full power to obtain probate of the will, but I wanted to pursue in London my discussions about joining the firm of Secker and Warburg. Beaverbrook even helped to book me a passage on the Queen Mary.

Meanwhile there was the problem of Sir Alexander Korda. Shortly after our 'row' over the dinner party Beaverbrook said to me: 'That fellow Korda, he's been here a week, can't you get him to go?' Later that very same day, Sir Alexander Korda confided to me in his delightful Anglo-Hungarian accent that he was bored to tears, but didn't want to offend his Lordship by leaving for no obvious reason. I managed to reassure him on that count and he left very soon afterwards.

With Pamela Churchill there was no such problem. She had youth, charm, gaiety, wit and great good looks. She spread these attributes impartially over Beaverbrook, Nockels and myself. To all three of us she was *persona gratissima*. She was also a member of a boating expedition at which, almost inadvertently, I chose my successor.

It was suggested by the acting Governor of the island, Sir William Addis, it was organized by someone whom I had first met three years previously. Her name was Joan Bright, and it was inevitable that she would organize any expedition, boating or otherwise, in which she took part. She was that sort of person. Joan had for most of the war been on the personal staff of Sir Hastings Ismay, the head of the military section of the War Cabinet Offices. As such, and because of her charm and efficiency, she had been detailed to arrange and supervise the social and accommodation problems of the camp followers – from the Chief of the Imperial General Staff downwards – who accompanied Churchill on his numerous trans-Atlantic voyages. I had first met her in 1943 on the Queen Mary, where at first I knew very few of my fellow-passengers, and where, by the time we reached Staten Island I knew, thanks to Joan, a great many. Now she was in wholly delightful control of the Governor's yacht.

Also on board was the Governor's ADC, a personable young man of obvious talent. The weather was sunny, the sea a mill pond, everyone, including Lord Beaverbrook, was in an expansive mood. Mine was over-expansive. Drawing Joan aside I confided to her that I was almost certainly going to desert my

master. 'Splendid,' Joan replied, 'then Laurence can succeed you.'
Laurence was nearing the end of his tour of duty as ADC. In
due course, partly on my recommendation, he did succeed me.
Alas! he had no George Malcolm Thomson to guide his initially
faltering footsteps; nor could he read aloud from the newspapers in a car without feeling sick.

Probably no transatlantic liner in history has had so many
devoted admirers as RMS Queen Mary, but in March 1946 she
was not at her best. As a troopship during the war her accommodation had been so redesigned that she could carry a complete division. Her reconversion to peace-time civilian use was
far from complete, and this time I was a private passenger, not
a member of a Churchill mission. Each cabin was fitted with
eight bunks, mine contained a more than an average comple-
ment of snorers. Still, there were compensations. Pamela
Churchill was on board, so was Victor Butler, so, fresh from his
triumphs as press attaché in Washington, was Isaiah Berlin.
Isaiah was a late riser, but he was worth waiting for. At about
half past six every evening he would make his first appearance
in the hall on the main deck. There he would entrance us with
unrivalled pyrotechnical outpourings on almost every subject
on earth. He was late again on the day we docked. In vain his
steward urged him to get on with his packing. In due course the
rest of the crowded ship assembled in the customs shed to find
our luggage under the appropriate letter of the alphabet.
Presently I noticed the rather shambling, anxious looking figure
of Mr Berlin. 'I can't find my luggage,' he said to me, peering
short-sightedly at the mound of it stacked under B. We tried
A, C, D to no avail; then a porter started moving trainwards,
and I followed. Later I saw Isaiah on the train. He was beaming.
'I'm a mystery figure,' he announced, 'I'm Mr X.' It was under
X that he had finally run his luggage to ground.

My master soon wearied of the somewhat fitful sunshine
and frequent high winds of Bermuda, and life with Beaverbrook
resumed its normal unpredictable course. At Cherkley Nockels
still reigned supreme, as at the *Daily Express* office did Arthur

Christiansen. At heart, a school prefect, he would put messages on the newspaper's notice board. 'Well done, we scooped the *Daily Mail*,' or 'Let me remind you, we must all pull together.' In his office next to mine, George Millar, harassed but extremely efficient, looked after the Lord's affairs. Perhaps his most harassed moment had been at Christmas 1941, when Beaverbrook had left for the Washington Conference without signing the Christmas present cheques. Loud were the wails that arose from the usual recipients, many of whom, myself included, had been relying on their arrival to keep their banks quiet. But for me there was now a difference. The financial and other details of becoming a publisher were completed soon after my return from Bermuda. There remained the decision of when to resign and what sort of letter of resignation to compile. I fixed on the beginning of September as my departure date. The letter suffered a number of birth pangs. It was a very difficult one to write. Over six years ago I had been an initially reluctant applicant for a job, now I was preparing to depart of my own volition. Both my entrance and exit denoted attitudes to which Beaverbrook was unaccustomed. He was fully versed in the art of getting rid of people, he had little experience of people getting rid of him. I was extremely anxious to retain friendly relations with a man to whom I owed so much and for whom, for all the criticisms I had mentally from time to time made of him, I had developed a deep admiration and real affection. How to contrive a letter which would achieve this objective? I compiled several drafts; the final version contained many an echo from those fourteen letters which Thomson and I had helped him to write to his Prime Minister in those days of 1940 to 1942. 'Proud to have served' (though I refrained from 'under your banner'), 'shall always remember the most exciting days of my life' (as I have been writing this book I have realized this was no less than the truth). I could hardly use 'my asthma' as an excuse, since he knew perfectly well I was a reasonably healthy individual. Inadvertently I hit on the one excuse for leaving him which would appeal to him. I wrote that I had now the chance to make good *on my own*.

At last, in mid-July, the letter was dispatched. It had been shown to no one but George Malcolm Thomson, who gave it his blessing. For forty-eight hours I waited in trepidation. How would this man who for many years had in fact dominated my life, react? The answer came in a telephone conversation.

'Anything new?'

'No, I don't think so.'

'That was a fine article of yours in the *Standard*.'

'Thank you, Sir.' (It had as usual been vetted and improved by him.)

'Those damn Tories are behaving just like Socialists.'

'I couldn't agree with you more' – it had been the theme of my article.

A slight pause, then: 'So you're going to leave me.'

'Yes.'

'I'd like you to tell me all about the new job.'

'I'd love to.'

'Come down to Cherkley this evening and tell me.'

A little later I confessed to E. J. Robertson, his newspapers' general manager, who for many years filled, as far as it could be filled, the post of Beaverbrook's right-hand man, that I had been scared of Beaverbrook's reaction.

'You needn't have worried,' he replied. 'If you had gone to the *Daily Mail*, or any other paper, he wouldn't have forgiven you. But to set out to make your own career, he'd never mind that. It's what he did himself.'

This was truly, if kindly, put. Beaverbrook had from boyhood earned and saved every penny (or cent) which later he was to use for his own advancement. Mine was a softer option. I had luckily inherited money which made it possible to strike out on my own.

A few weeks before I was due to leave a leading literary agent came in to the *Daily Express* offices, bearing with him a synopsis of a book which he suggested would make a good serial. I happened to catch a glimpse of it. The book would be written by an unknown Major in the Canadian Army, who had been given the task of interviewing German officers captured on the Western Front. It seemed to me a brilliant synopsis, and I alerted my future publishing partners, suggesting that they made a substantial offer for the book rights. They did so, and so surprised was the literary agent that they had even heard of it that he accepted the offer. The book was called *Defeat in the West*. It is still a reference book and has sold many thousand copies. Its author has become famous in more than one field. His name is Milton Shulman. When the book was published in 1947 I sent a copy to Beaverbrook. He asked me to go to see him. 'It's first rate,' he told me, 'I'm much obliged to you for sending it to me. Where's the author now?' I gave him Shulman's address. He phoned the Editor of the *Evening Standard*. 'Ever heard of a fellow called Milton Shulman?' Apparently the answer was negative, because: 'Well, get hold of him and hire him at once.'

A week before I was due to leave his employment Beaverbrook summoned me to his London flat. There he cross-questioned me closely.

'This firm of yours, is it making money?'

'Yes, Sir, quite a lot.'

'Have your lawyers looked at its books?'

'Yes, closely.'

'Have you put all your money into it?'

'No, not all of it.'

'What would happen if the firm went broke? Would you be able to live?'

'In reduced circumstances, yes.'

'But you'd be hard up.'

'Yes, but I'd have enough to live on. I could get another job.'

'You're sure of that?'

'Yes, quite sure.'

He picked up his dictaphone, rasped into it: 'Mr Millar, you can cut Mr Farrer out of my will.'

13

AFTER THE PARTING

FIVE THOUSAND POUNDS had gone down the drain. There was no sort of reason, since I was leaving him of my own volition, why I should have remained in his will. Yet on reflection I realized that it could easily have been otherwise. A different answer to one of his questions was all that was required. 'What would happen if the firm went broke? Would you be able to live?' 'Well, actually no.' 'Mr Millar, you can *keep* Mr Farrer in my will.' Security – and bondage. Not, as was to happen quite often in the future, a telephone message asking if I could dine with him, but a different sort of message, commanding me to dine at short notice. I should have been in his debt – a puppet on a string – and he would have taken advantage of the fact. Since I am still reasonably solvent I am glad I answered as I did.

Shortly after I left him he asked me to write an appreciation of his old friend Lord Dowding, timed to coincide with the anniversary of the Battle of Britain. Its appearance in the *Sunday Express* provoked a telephone call from Cherkley. There were three agreeable features about this call. First he congratulated me on the article, then he asked me how much the *Sunday Express* had paid me. I replied 'Fifty pounds' to which he answered 'I'll make them double it'; finally, for the first time in six and a half years he called me 'David'. I was absurdly pleased, but I never called him 'Max'. It would have been too like calling God Almighty by his Christian name. With this unexpected bonus in my pocket I left for a holiday in Portugal.

During the next few years the firm of Secker and Warburg seemed to outsiders to be prospering. Our publications were

widely reviewed. Milton Shulman's *Defeat in the West* was
an undoubted success, George Orwell's *Animal Farm*, rejected
by several publishers in 1944 because it was anti-Russian, had
become a best-seller, Gabriel Chevallier's bawdy epic about a
French public convenience was continuing its triumphant
career. But our accountants, our bankers took a different view.
During the war publishers had been allocated a paper ration
based on their pre-war output. My colleagues had confidently
believed that this rationing would be abolished soon after the
war ended. In this expectation they had increased both the
staff and the capital of the company. But four years later paper
rationing was still in existence. The number of books which we
could produce and sell, however well reviewed, was insufficient
to cover the firm's overheads, let alone pay dividends. I had
joined the firm on an exiguous salary, there was no possibility
of its being increased. My private capital began to vanish at
an alarming rate.

During these years I had seen a good deal of Beaverbrook.
He had shown much interest in the fortunes of Secker and Warburg, and had, I learned later, told his newspapers to give
maximum attention to the books we published. Now I went to
see him, told him the true facts, and, risking bondage after all,
asked for his help. He did not hesitate; he told me that he would
ask (for 'ask' read of course 'tell') his newspapers to commission
occasional articles, book and theatre reviews from me and put
me on their payroll for a year, at a salary which solved all my
immediate financial problems. Nor did bondage ensue. He made
no demands on me. If I sat drinking with him, often stark naked,
in his roof garden overlooking Green Park, it was at his
invitation not command, as was a delightfully farcical weekend
at Cherkley when a house party gathered to watch a troupe of
foreign dancers dance on the lawn in a downpour of rain. But
Cherkley was not the same. Nockels, the great Nockels, no
longer presided there. He had moved onwards and upwards to
grander situations. He had left a great gap. For me life as a
personal secretary without him would have been far less entertaining, a good deal more difficult. He had been a splendid com-

panion in adversity, and with whom to laugh at the farcical situation which befell us.

After resigning as Beaverbrook's major-domo he was employed for a time in sorting and arranging his ex-master's private papers, housed in the vaults of the Daily Express building. He could be seen, proceeding daily down Fleet Street, immaculate in striped trousers and bowler hat, albeit these were somewhat untypical Fleet Street garb. Thence he moved on to be head valet at the Carlton Club. There, on one occasion, he took a cup of early morning tea to an elderly Tory peer, Earl Winterton. The Earl demanded: 'Draw the curtains and tell me what the day is like.' Nockels complied. 'It looks as if it would be fine, *Sir*.'

'I am accustomed to being called "My Lord".'

'I worked for six years for Prince Arthur of Connaught; *He* never objected to being addressed as "Sir".'

Collapse of elderly peer, with whom Nockels subsequently became very friendly.

During this time Nockels was developing an increasing interest in spiritualism, particularly in its potentiality for healing. He is now Vice-President of the Union of Spiritualist Mediums and Trustee of its Benevolent Fund. He 'gives healing' each week at the Spiritual Association of Great Britain. He remains his own inimitable self.

During this period of salaried odd-job man I was given a variety of assignments, from which I learned at least one lesson. The more time one was given to write an article or review a book or play the more unsuccessful it was likely to be. I was sent a book about Marshal Tito three weeks before it was due to be published. The review was of a tedium that still makes me ashamed. I was given less than twelve hours to review Kingsley Martin's book on Harold Laski and received a letter of congratulation from the Editor of the *Sunday Express* for calling Laski, John Strachey, Kingsley Martin and Victor Gollancz 'the four pink horsemen of the apocalypse'. On another occasion a book about Ernest Bevin reached me at five o'clock one Saturday evening with a demand that I telephone my five-hundred-word review by seven-thirty at latest. There was only one answer to this problem. I looked up 'Beaverbrook' in the index and constructed my review entirely around the references to him. It met in the highest quarter with a measure of approval.

After a while the clouds began to lift from the fortunes of Secker and Warburg. Paper rationing was at last abolished. In a single year the firm published two best-sellers, George Orwell's *Nineteen Eighty Four* and Alberto Moravia's *A Woman of Rome*. My own salary could be raised. I went to Beaverbrook, told him of the new situation, said I no longer needed the salary, though I would of course work off the unearned balance of it by writing for him whenever he required it. He waved this aside, told me he was glad my firm was doing well, asked me to stay to dinner.

It was three years later that he asked me for advice. 'Tell me,' he said, over a drink at his Arlington House flat, 'what do you think about Driberg?'

The sycophant, never wholly absent, I am afraid, in my dealings with him, rose to the surface. 'I owe him at least one debt of gratitude; he introduced me to you.'

'Apart from that' – he wasn't immune to sycophancy – 'as a person.'

'I like him very much.'

'And a writer?'

'He's a first-class journalist.'

'He's writing a book about me. He's asked me for any help with private papers, personal reminiscences. Should I give it?'

I took a deep plunge. 'You've often told me, Sir, that you'd like to be remembered "warts and all". Like Cromwell.' I added, remembering that he was one of his heroes.

'God damn it, David, all I want is an honest portrait.'

'That, I'm sure, Tom will give you. But I think there will be some warts.'

He made no answer to this, but changed the subject. But he did give Tom Driberg a considerable measure of assistance.

In 1956 the book was published. I thought it on the whole unfair to its subject, exaggerating the warts, minimizing the achievements, though to be fair to the author he had not worked intimately with Beaverbrook during his greatest days. Months earlier a proof copy had been sent Beaverbrook at his house in Jamaica. He took it to bed with him. Next morning, on the evidence of one of his guests, he came down to breakfast, slammed the copy on the table and declaimed : 'Man has been falling ever since the birth of Adam. But never in the whole course of human history has any man fallen quite as low as that fellow Driberg.' He fully approved of the hostile review I later wrote of the book, and wrote to tell me so.

During the last ten years of his life he spent increasing periods in search of sunshine in the Bahamas, Jamaica or the South of France – with fleeting visits to New Brunswick where he took much pleasure in supervising his many benefactions to the University at his native Fredericton. I saw him less frequently in consequence – an invitation to cross the Atlantic to be present at the opening of the University's new library did not, alas! include the fare. On each of his birthdays I sent him a telegram and received a friendly letter in reply. His health, I knew, was deteriorating, but his mental faculties remained unimpaired. On one occasion, when Beaverbrook was eighty, Thomson was summoned to stay at the villa in the South of France. The only other guest was Sir Winston Churchill, who on the first night retired to bed immediately after dinner. Thereupon Beaverbrook started to reminisce. Four hours later they retired to bed. For all that time, Thomson told me, he had listened completely enthralled as the inside story of a pageant of history was unrolled in a manner which the written word could never excel. The struggle over the House of Lords in 1911 – the unexpected emergence as leader of the Tory Party of his fellow Canadian, Bonar Law; the approach to civil war in Ireland in 1914, spear-headed by F. E. Smith (later Lord Birkenhead) and Sir Edward Carson; all the main figures of World War I; how Lloyd George became Prime Minister; Austen Chamberlain and Locarno; Baldwin, Ramsay MacDonald, and the Gold Standard; the Abdication; the Munich Crisis; much that even Thomson didn't know about the conduct of World War II; and, of course, above all the other guest now asleep upstairs. As he listened to the unfolding story, Thomson realized that here was a very great film script; these figures, these dramas, passed before his eyes as if there was a 'Vistavision' screen at the end of the dining room.

Two years had passed without my seeing him when I received a letter asking me how I was getting on, telling me he had heard good things of my firm and that he would very much like to see me again. Would I come and dine with him? I replied at once, on a Friday, that I would very much like to dine with him any night the following week except Monday, when I had promised to take a friend to the opera. When I reached my office next Monday there was a message awaiting me: Would I dine with him that night? I rang up his secretary, explaining that I had told him this was the *one* night that I was engaged. 'Yes,' he replied wearily, 'I know.' I refused the invitation. It was perhaps a last flick of the whip, a subconscious desire that his ex-secretary would be prepared to throw over a previous engagement in order to dine with his ex-boss. Had I known then that I should never see him again I have no doubt that I would have 'chucked' and offended my opera guest.

Though this book is intended simply as a personal memoir, I have tried to analyse and synthesize my feelings about the career of this many-sided man. In a memorable passage in his *Short History of England* G. K. Chesterton thus describes the hitherto unknown Henry Tudor, who at the battle of Bosworth Field in 1485 defeated Richard III of England and founded the famous dynasty that bears his name: 'A wanderer from the Welsh Marches, a nobody from nowhere who found the crown of England under a bush of thorns.' When William Maxwell Aitken arrived in England in 1910 he was to the British people, so far as they were aware of him at all, 'a wanderer from the hinterland of New Brunswick, a nobody from nowhere'. His rise in his adopted country was meteoric, his power and influence in some respects very great, yet never did they consider awarding him a crown or even, save for one epic year, their complete confidence.

The reason, I believe, is that he never won the allegiance of the British middle classes, and it was this bourgeoisie that throughout the years of his active career were the dominant factor on the British political scene. He was a free enterprise man, well and good, but he was also an opponent of tradition and privilege in all its forms, and this was intolerable. He was a radical capitalist, and this to the middle classes was a contradiction in terms. Again, his belief in the Empire was passionately sincere; he could be excused for thinking this would win him wide support among those whose public-school forefathers had founded it, but he never realized that 'Rule Britannia' had ceased to be sung with any real fervour after the Boer War. Lastly, his methods of political warfare, both in his newspapers and on the platform, were considered vulgar and 'un-British'. Many a country squire and his bazaar-opening lady never forgave him for inventing the gossip column. The middle classes as a whole never forgave him for the campaign he waged against their beloved Mr Baldwin in the thirties; in World War II many regarded him as Churchill's evil genius.

So the 'nobody from nowhere' became 'somebody' indeed – a man whose character, activities and achievements will be discussed long after most of his contemporaries have faded into oblivion, a man who revolutionized British journalism and who wrote two books which will be source material for students of World War I for all time, a man who played a decisive part in saving Britain in the summer of 1940. But politically he got relatively nowhere.

Could it have been otherwise? The answer must be no. Beaverbrook possessed an exceptional brain, great powers of concentration and of inspiring others, immense drive; he was adept at solving an immediate problem. But the long view too often escaped him and his vision was anyway too often clouded by prejudice. Personally he was capable, as this book has shown, of great generosity and kindness, but he lacked magnanimity; a slight or insult, real or unintentional, was not easily forgotten. It has been frequently alleged that each of his newspapers possessed a 'black book' in which were inscribed two classes of enemies, those who must be constantly attacked and those who must be totally ignored. I never saw these books and they were probably legendary, but the legend underlined a certain truth; he was not a forgiving man.

These were grave handicaps in the pursuit of 'the crown', which in his eyes was the premiership. Gravest of all was the fact that for the British electorate he was altogether too strong meat. Throughout the century they had been inured to having gentlemen as Prime Ministers. Only at the nadir of Britain's fortunes in World War I did they turn to Lloyd George, the one exception. Ramsay MacDonald, first Labour Prime Minister in 1924, as if by instinct started to hobnob with duchesses. The replacement of 'gentleman' Chamberlain in 1940 was by 'gentleman-genius' Churchill. To his credit Beaverbrook had very little use for gentlemen as such. To the discredit of the British middle classes they were so obsessed by the strident unorthodoxy of this Canadian interloper on their political stage that they consistently underestimated his qualities and magnified his defects. That in my view he had neither the balance of intellect and judgement nor the staying power to lead the country is in this context beside the point. There are people today who still regard him as a fairly close approximation of the devil. If so, then I was at least half in love with Satan.

On the eve of his eighty-fifth birthday I sent him my customary telegram which, according to his reply, encouraged and amused him. I had quoted to him the remark of one of his favourite musical comedy actresses of the twenties, Maisie Gay: 'It doesn't matter how old you are, it's just how young you feel.' The occasion was marked by a celebration dinner given by Lord Thomson, his fellow-Canadian who had by now also built up a newspaper empire. At the Dorchester there gathered one hundred and fifty guests representing every spectrum of Britain's political and social life, from left-wing Socialists to right-wing Tories, from personal secretaries to dukes and duchesses. The whole company knew that the guest of honour was a sick man – those who had earlier seen him interviewed on television in his Cherkley garden had been shocked by his appearance. Some knew that he was dying, only a few knew that he was dying in great pain from a cancer of the bone and had wondered if he would be able to attend. He walked on the arm of his son slowly up the banqueting hall, took his seat, and the meal proceeded. At last it was time for him to reply to the toast of the guest of honour. Beaverbrook rose and with scarcely a reference to his notes, in a voice as strong as it had ever been, made one of the great speeches of his life. He spoke of journalism, of its tasks, its duties, its rewards, its ambitions, its scope for the younger generation, of what it should and could mean in the life of a nation. The speech, full of that humorous barbed malice of which he was a master, defiant in its overtones, lasted half an hour. As he sat down the banqueting hall rose to him. 'For he's a jolly good fellow' sang in unison such disparate characters as Michael Foot and the Earl of Rosebery. 'For he's a jolly good fellow' sang Cabinet Ministers past and present, old colleagues from the MAP days, politicians and businessmen from the United States and the Dominions, members of his editorial staffs. As he left the hall, again on the arm of the son of whom he was so proud and who, he knew now, would very soon succeed him, there was on his face that impish grin which I had seen so often when he had brought off a pet project or worsted an enemy.

In this case the enemy, of course, was not to be long denied. A fortnight later he was dead. But he had gone out not with a whimper but with a bang.

INDEX

Ackerley, J. R., 17
Addis, Sir William, 159
Aitken, Janet, 137
Aitken, Max, 50-1, 126-7, 137, 172
Albert, 12, 20-1, 27, 31, 37, 51
Alexander, A. V., 138-9
Alexander, General, 127, 142
Amery, Leo, 34
Arnaud, Yvonne, 107
Asquith, Margot, 19
Attlee, Clement, 84-5, 140, 143-4, 146, 150

Baldwin, Stanley, 139, 168, 170
Beaverbrook, Lady, 31
Beaverbrook, Lord:
March-April 1940:
11-14, 18-32
May 1940-April 1941:
Minister of Aircraft Production, 35-67; Minister of State, 67-8
May 1941-April 1943:
Minister of Supply, 69-73, 74-5 (at Placentia Bay), 75-6 (in Moscow), 77, 78-9 (in Washington); Minister of Production, 80-1, 82-3 (resignation); 84-97 (Washington Mission), 98-100 ('Second Front'), 101-110, 111 (Leader of House of Lords), 112-19 (in Washington), 120
October 1943-May 1945:
Lord Privy Seal, 121-3, 124-8 (Marrakesh), 129-33, 134-5 (Washington), 136-9, 140 (Yalta), 141-2

After 1945:
143-5 (election campaign), 148-50, 151 (Paris), 152, 153-60 (in Bermuda), 161-71, 172 (last speech)
Bennett, Captain, 57
Bennett, Lord, 58, 66, 105
Berle, Adolf, 128-9, 132, 135
Berlin, Isaiah, 132, 160
Bevan, Aneurin, 103, 143
Beveridge, Sir William, 137
Bevin, Ernest, 55, 64, 81, 84, 101, 143-4, 149-50, 166
Bickell, J. P., 57-8, 66, 117-8, 158
Birkenhead, Lord, 168
Bracken, Brendan, 85-6, 89, 98, 105, 123, 138-9, 145
Bridges, Sir Edward, 80
Bright, Joan, 159-60
Brooke, Sir Alan, 113
Brown, Sir William, 73, 77
Brown, W. J., 139
Brownlow, Lord, 36
Buchman, Dr Frank, 19, 29
Burns, Robert, 73
Butler, Victor, 134-5, 156, 160

Carson, Sir Edward, 168
Castlerosse, Lord, 18, 36, 105, 137, 152
Chamberlain, Austen, 168
Chamberlain, Neville, 22, 30-1, 34, 40, 74, 131, 153, 171
Channon, Sir Henry, 152
Chiang-Kai-Shek, Mme, 118
Christiansen, Arthur, 29-30, 102-3, 151, 156, 161